EPIC
30-MINUTE
ROASTS

MAJA ZVER & JERNEJ ZVER

Founders of Jernej Kitchen

PAGE STREET
PUBLISHING CO.

PAGE STREET
PUBLISHING CO.

DEDICATION

To our readers and food community, you are the kindest people.

This book wouldn't be possible without you—thank you for your support, and thank you for recreating recipes and sharing them with your loved ones and via social media with the world.

CONTENTS

JUICY POULTRY FOR ANY OCCASION

EPIC PORK MADE IN NO TIME

IT'S BRUNCH O'CLOCK

HANDS-OFF SWEET TREATS

ESSENTIAL SAUCES

Introduction

We come from a small country called Slovenia. Living in a small country with a population of a little over 2 million people has its cons, but it also has its pros, especially when it comes to food. We are blessed to be surrounded by high-quality ingredients, grass-fed animals, and many organic farms. At home, we have two large vegetable gardens and more than ten fruit trees.

Being inspired by what's in season helps us develop new recipes, and it helps us get the most flavor out of produce. We try to follow that philosophy in life, on our blog, Jernej Kitchen, and in this book, too.

Over the years, we found that roasting isn't reserved for autumn and winter: This simple cooking technique can help extract a lot of flavor from spring and summer fruits and vegetables, too.

To us, the flavor is the most important thing when it comes to cooking. And, when we have a lot of time, achieving deep and intense flavors is an easy job. But when we are short on time, it almost seems impossible to get the most delicious meal in under 30 minutes. Well, it is possible. Incorporating simple techniques—such as searing the meat before roasting it in the oven or broiling it to get a crunchy and crispy exterior—helps with just that. Marinades are reserved for weekends and celebrations. Coating the meat or vegetables in a mixture of spices helps develop aromatic flavors in much less time. Last but not least, taking those extra five minutes to make a sauce is life-changing and can turn almost any simple dish into an extraordinary one.

Over the years and after many, many hours spent in the professional kitchen, Jernej also changed his perspective on garnishes. Sometimes a drizzle of high-quality olive oil or a sprinkle of chopped cilantro for freshness or chopped nuts for texture can make all the difference. Sure, we eat with our mouths, but we also eat with our eyes, and, when you can satisfy them both, you have won.

Roasting is the perfect way to prepare lunch or dinner during the week and on weekends, too. All you need to do is choose a recipe, harvest or buy the ingredients, prepare them, and let the oven do all the work. We hope that this book will be a useful tool for you to create quick, delicious, and effortless meals for yourself and your family.

How to Use This Book

Roasting may sound hard or complicated to some, but, in reality, it just means cooking on a high temperature in the oven to get the most flavor, juiciness, and aroma from the dish. In fact, roasting is easy because you don't need a lot of skills, and there isn't a lot of effort involved in this type of cooking. Your oven does most of the work. But with that being said, there are some things that we should mention that are pretty specific to roasting on high temperatures.

Not all ovens are the same, which means that they all work in their own way, so keeping an eye on the food that is roasting in the oven, especially food being broiled, is essential. Start by always reading the whole recipe first, then continue with preheating your oven and using an oven thermometer to check if the oven is preheated to the desired temperature.

While the oven is preheating, start preparing all of the ingredients needed for the recipe. The meat should always be used at room temperature, which means you need to take it out of the fridge at least 15 to 20 minutes before starting the recipe. If you are buying fresh meat, don't worry about this step; by the time you get home from the butcher, your meat will be ready.

In this book, we use smaller cuts of meat and vegetables that are thinly sliced or cut into cubes. The roasting time is short, so choosing the right size and thickness of the ingredients is fundamental for success.

Now let's start cooking. When you have all of your ingredients ready to use, also known as *mise en place*, and the oven is preheated, we can start following the recipe step by step.

When roasting meat, it is essential to note that all the beef, lamb, and game recipes in this book are cooked to medium-rare, and all the pork recipes are cooked to medium. That is our personal preference; however, we included the internal temperatures for rare, medium-rare, medium, and well-done meat, too. So, using an instant-read thermometer, you can make sure that the meat is done according to your taste. After the meat is roasted, allow it some time to rest. That way, it will continue cooking and developing flavors.

Most of the dishes in this book are cooked in the center of the oven, on the middle rack, but some are broiled on the top rack. When broiling on the top rack, there is immense heat coming from the top of the oven, so it is especially important to keep an eye on the food, for example, when making Lemon Chicken Kebabs (page 63). Most of the dishes are only finished under the broiler, to get a caramelized top or some extra crispiness.

We are working with high temperatures, so make sure to use protective kitchen gloves when placing an ovenproof skillet in the oven or when taking the baking sheet with the food from the oven. We wrap a kitchen towel around an ovenproof skillet once it's out of the oven, because we tend to forget how hot it is.

Follow the recipe, but also use your eyes and gut feeling. Roasting can yield different results depending on your oven, cut of meat, how thick the vegetables are, and what pans you use. Remember, color equals flavor.

PANTRY

It's always easier to cook when your pantry is stocked with the essentials. We like to have rice, dried pasta, spices, legumes, and different condiments on hand at all times. Weekly, we stock up on vegetables, fruits, meat, and fish to keep those foods fresh and seasonal. Buying seasonally is not only more affordable: It is the tastiest, too. We know that everyone has their preference when it comes to ingredients, but here are a few things to keep in mind when you shop for ingredients to use in the recipes in this book.

BUTTER: Always use unsalted butter for recipes in this cookbook. You can season to taste with salt in the end. Use high-quality, high-fat-content butter.

STOCKS: You will find chicken or beef stocks in many of these recipes. You can always substitute them with water if you don't have stock available. However, we recommend trying to keep good-quality, low-sodium stocks in your pantry.

HONEY: We always choose floral or acacia honey for this great natural sweetener because they are mild and don't have an intense flavor.

OILS: We couldn't live without high-quality olive oil, and, in our humble opinion, it's definitely worth investing in. For cooking, you can always use a cheaper olive oil. But for dressings, drizzling, and finishing touches, use the best-quality oil; it brings out the best in a dish. Along with olive oil, stock a canola oil with a high smoke point and sesame oil for Asian-inspired recipes.

VINEGARS: Stock apple cider, rice, sherry, white wine, and balsamic vinegars. They are all delicious and specific and work wonders in all those tasty dressings. However, don't stress out if you don't have a particular vinegar at home; simply substitute with the one that you have on hand.

SOY SAUCE: For all Asian-inspired dishes, soy sauce is a must. It helps develop the umami flavor and adds a bit of saltiness to the dish. We always use a low-sodium, light soy sauce that doesn't overpower the dish. If you aren't using light soy sauce, thin the sauce with water.

BREADCRUMBS: We use panko and dried breadcrumbs the most. Feel free to use homemade breadcrumbs, too.

WINE: We use wines for cooking quite often. Don't worry; in these recipes, the alcohol always evaporates, so you are left only with the flavor. That's why it's essential to choose the right wine. It doesn't need to be pricey. We use Moscato, Vin Santo, white Port, Riesling, Madeira, and Marsala, as these sweet wines are well suited for the short cooking times of our recipes. We use Chardonnay when the recipe calls for a drier wine.

CITRUS: Citrus juices add so much flavor and freshness to dishes. Always use freshly squeezed citrus juice and unwaxed fruits for lemon, lime, or orange zest.

MISO: This traditional Japanese ingredient is packed with umami flavor. We always use dark miso paste, but feel free to use light or dark.

SALT: We always use sea salt for cooking but choose fleur de sel or a flaky salt for delicate finishes. We recommend using the salt you are most familiar with for seasoning.

PEPPER: Freshly ground black pepper is the way to go because it's the most flavorful.

PARSLEY: Use fresh flat-leaf parsley, also called Italian parsley, for seasoning and garnishes.

SHALLOTS AND ONIONS: Shallots are sweeter than onions, are more flavorful, and need a shorter time to cook. This makes them the perfect onion substitute when you are trying to save time. However, feel free to substitute with onion. When it comes to onions, we always use brown onions for cooking, unless otherwise noted.

EQUIPMENT

You don't need a lot, and you definitely don't need expensive cooking equipment to create good food. We would encourage you to invest in a high-quality, ovenproof skillet and a few baking sheets, along with a sharp chef's knife. Everything else is optional, though other items listed here help you achieve good results faster and easier. Along with a good blender or immersion blender, this is the equipment that we used most often for this book.

BAKING SHEET: We use stainless steel or aluminum rimmed baking sheets for most of the roasts in this book. If it's not specified, don't use parchment paper because roasting directly on baking sheets allows the meat or vegetable to cook faster. If possible, invest in one large baking sheet, called a half-sheet pan, and one small baking sheet, a quarter-sheet pan.

BAKING DISH: Deep baking dishes are great for roasting meat or vegetables with sauces or liquids. Use metal baking dishes or roasting pans when possible, because the food tends to cook quicker, thanks to the faster conduction of heat. Also, many of our recipes call for broiling, and metal baking dishes are safer for that method.

DUTCH OVEN POT: Dutch ovens are an excellent investment, because they serve you for years and can be used for all kinds of cooking, including slow roasting or for roasts that are made in a short period of time, as in this book. The thick walls of the pot allow the ingredients to cook evenly and quickly. We love using our 5½-quart (10¼-inch [26-cm] diameter) round Dutch oven. Both Le Creuset and Staub make good ones.

OVENPROOF SKILLET: We use stainless steel skillets and cast-iron skillets—our 10-inch (26-cm) is our most used—almost every day. They are perfect for when you divide the cooking process between cooking on the stove and roasting in the oven. But be careful to use ovenproof stainless-steel skillets without a plastic handle.

OVENPROOF NONSTICK PAN: When it comes to cooking fish, a nonstick pan is the way to go. Fish can stick to the pan very quickly, and having a nonstick pan can prevent that from happening. We usually use nonstick pans for sauces and searing meat, too.

MANDOLINE SLICER AND GRATER: A mandoline slicer is such a good investment. It will save you a lot of time, and roasting will be so much easier thanks to the evenly sliced vegetables. For this book, we mostly used a Microplane grater, which is perfect for finely grating citrus, cheese, garlic, and ginger.

KNIVES: A large chef's knife is excellent for cutting and chopping; it is the most-used tool in our kitchen. Then, we also recommend getting a good carving knife for meat.

THERMOMETERS: An instant-read thermometer is the way to go. It helps you check the temperature of the meat and fish instantly so that you can ensure the doneness of the meat according to your taste. An instant-read thermometer also enables you to ensure that the temperature of the fish and meat is in the safe zone. For recipes in this book, we don't recommend using meat thermometers because they tend to take too long to show the right temperature. An oven thermometer will help you make sure that the oven is correctly preheated before you roast your food.

METAL TONGS: This tool is an extension of your hands. They are instrumental when turning or flipping meat or vegetables while they are roasting in the oven, as well as for placing seared meat on a baking dish.

PEELER: A good speed peeler or Y peeler is essential for quick and easy peeling of soft and hard vegetables and fruits.

TIMER: When roasting on high temperatures, it is crucial to use a timer to make sure the dishes are properly cooked. We often use Alexa or Siri on our iPhones, so there's no need to get fancy and buy a pricey timer. You probably have one on hand already.

PROTECTIVE GLOVES: We work with high temperatures in this book, so use protective kitchen gloves when handling hot pans and baking sheets.

SUCCULENT BEEF, LAMB, AND GAME IN HALF THE TIME

So, what do beef, lamb, and game have in common? Two things. First is the addictive aroma wafting through the house while the meat is roasting. It is so specific, so rich, so comforting, and so hearty; there really is nothing better than roasting. And second, we need a good kitchen thermometer to check the doneness of these meats so it totally matches our preference and taste.

We wanted to incorporate as many different cuts of meat as possible in this chapter, and we love the diverse recipes. We have Mini Meatloaves (page 21), glazed with ketchup and BBQ sauce, that are made in less than 30 minutes and make the perfect holiday centerpiece. Then, there's a beautiful Rack of Lamb with Mediterranean Herbs (page 26) that celebrates high-quality meat and the simplicity of a good roast, with just a few ingredients. You will fall in love with incredibly tender Soft Italian Meatballs (page 37), which are best served with spaghetti or mashed potatoes for a simple yet incredibly hearty and comforting weeknight dinner. Last but not least, we love recipes like the London Broil Beef Steak (page 29), where we have a very cheap, rough cut of meat that is transformed into a fancy dinner by using the right technique.

When it comes to roasting beef, lamb, and game, it all comes down to using the right cut of meat, choosing the proper roasting technique, and keeping an eye on that internal temperature. Like all other recipes in this book, these too are made in less than 30 minutes.

SUNDAY ROAST RIB EYE STEAK

SERVES 4

PREP TIME: 8 minutes

ROASTING TIME: 20–25 minutes

STEAK

1½–2 lbs (680–900 g) bone-in rib eye steak, 1½ inches (3 cm) thick, trimmed and tied

3 tbsp (45 ml) canola oil, divided

Salt and freshly ground black pepper

1 tbsp (14 g) unsalted butter

1 clove garlic, crushed

FOR SERVING

Bread and Horseradish Sauce (page 228), optional

This is as traditional as it gets: a simple piece of high-quality beef, roasted to perfection. Typically, you would first sear the steak and then roast it, but in this case, we roast the steak in the oven first and then sear it for a few minutes in a hot pan. By doing that, we ensure a beautiful, brown crust, while the meat remains juicy, soft, and delicious inside. Slice the rib eye thinly, sprinkle it with salt, and devour it. This Sunday roast is great for winter holidays, weekend gatherings, or fancy weeknight dinner dates. Serve it with Crispy Roasted Potatoes (page 171) and Roasted Root Vegetables (page 168).

Arrange a rack in the middle of the oven, then preheat it to 450°F (230°C).

For the steak, place the rib eye on a baking sheet. Drizzle with 1 tablespoon (15 ml) of oil per side. Generously season the steak with salt and pepper, and put the baking sheet on the middle rack of the oven. Roast for 10 minutes, then turn the steak and roast it for 10 to 15 minutes, or until the steak reaches the preferred temperature.

Before removing the rib eye from the oven, check the temperature of the steak. Insert a thermometer into the thickest part of the meat. For rare, the thermometer should register 125°F (52°C); for medium-rare, it should be 130°F (54°C); for medium, it should read 140°F (60°C); and for well-done, 155°F (68°C).

Place a pan over medium-high heat. When the pan is smoking hot, add the remaining 1 tablespoon (15 ml) of oil and transfer the steak from the oven to the pan. Sear the steak for about 2 minutes on each side. When you turn the steak, add the butter and garlic to the pan. Remove the pan from the heat, and let the steak rest for about 5 minutes.

To serve, top the steak with the horseradish sauce, if using.

SIMPLE TENDERLOIN ROAST

This is one showstopping centerpiece—a simple tenderloin roast that always impresses with its beautiful, perfectly roasted exterior and juicy interior. It's incredibly easy to make a tenderloin roast to your liking. Use a thermometer to check the temperature of the meat before taking it out of the oven to make sure it's done to your taste and preference. We prefer it medium-rare. Serve this for special occasions or a quick midweek dinner along with cooked asparagus and Crispy Roasted Potatoes (page 171).

SERVES 4

PREP TIME: 12 minutes

ROASTING TIME:
15–18 minutes

BEEF

4 lbs (1.8 kg) beef tenderloin
Salt and freshly ground black pepper
1 tbsp (15 ml) canola oil
1 tbsp (14 g) unsalted butter
2 cloves garlic, crushed
1 sprig fresh rosemary

FOR SERVING

Fleur de sel, optional
Bread and Horseradish Sauce
(page 228), optional

Arrange a rack in the middle of the oven, then preheat it to 410°F (210°C).

For the beef, pat the meat dry using paper towels. Cut the tenderloin in half crosswise to get two smaller fillets. Using kitchen string, tie the beef every 2 inches (4 cm). Season the meat with salt and pepper.

Place an ovenproof skillet over high heat. When the skillet is smoking hot, add the canola oil and the fillets. Sear the meat on all sides, 1 to 2 minutes per side, or 6 to 8 minutes in total. Sear one fillet at a time if the skillet is not large enough to hold the meat without crowding. Add the butter, garlic, and rosemary, and cook for a minute.

Transfer the seared meat to a baking sheet. Place it in the oven on the middle rack. Roast the meat for 15 to 18 minutes, turning the beef twice while roasting.

Before removing it from the oven, check the temperature of the meat. Insert a thermometer into the thickest part of the meat. For rare, the thermometer should register 125°F (52°C); for medium-rare, it should be 130°F (54°C); for medium, it should read 140°F (60°C); and for well-done, 155°F (68°C). Set the meat aside to rest for 5 to 10 minutes before serving.

To serve, slice the tenderloin roast, divide it among plates, and sprinkle the beef with the fleur de sel, if using. Top the slices with the horseradish sauce, if using.

SIMPLE BEEF ROAST

SERVES 4

PREP TIME: 14 minutes

ROASTING TIME:
12–14 minutes

BEEF

2 lbs (900 g) beef top round, top sirloin
cap (picanha), or tri-tip
1 tbsp (15 ml) olive oil
1 tbsp (15 ml) yellow mustard
Salt and freshly ground black pepper
1 tbsp (15 ml) canola oil

FOR SERVING

Olive oil
Freshly squeezed lemon juice

This simple beef roast recipe is created for all medium-rare steak lovers. It will only be succulent and tender if we prepare it medium-rare; otherwise, expect dry results that won't make you happy. This beef roast is juicy and delicious, and it could be served warm for dinner or served cold, cut in thin slices, as an appetizer for dinner dates or gatherings. Serve the beef with a slice of fresh or grilled bread and a simple arugula salad. For some extra flavoring, sprinkle the beef with pomegranate seeds.

Arrange a rack in the middle of the oven, then preheat it to 450°F (230°C).

For the beef, put the meat in a bowl. Drizzle it with the olive oil and season it with the mustard, salt, and pepper. Rub the mixture into the meat.

Place an ovenproof pan over high heat. When the pan is hot, add the canola oil and beef to the pan. Lower the heat to medium-high. Sear the meat on all four sides, 2 minutes per side, moving it around from time to time. The meat will become beautifully charred.

Roast the meat on the middle rack of the oven for 12 to 14 minutes, or until a thermometer inserted into the thickest part of the meat registers 120°F (48°C).

Remove the beef from the oven, and set it aside to rest for 10 minutes.

To serve, cut the beef against the grain into very thin slices. Drizzle the beef with the olive oil and some lemon juice.

NOTE: If you plan on making this simple beef roast for a cold appetizer, feel free to make it up to 3 days ahead. Let the roast beef come to room temperature after roasting it, then store it in an airtight container in the fridge.

MINI MEATLOAVES

SERVES 4

PREP TIME: 10 minutes

ROASTING TIME:
20–25 minutes

MEATLOAF

2 slices stale white bread, crusts removed and bread cut into cubes

⅓ cup (80 ml) warm milk

1 lb (450 g) ground beef chuck

1 shallot or ½ onion, finely diced

1 tbsp (5 g) chopped fresh parsley

1 tbsp (15 ml) Worcestershire sauce

½ tsp garlic powder

1 egg yolk

Salt and freshly ground black pepper

2 tbsp (12 g) panko breadcrumbs, optional

1 tbsp (15 ml) olive oil

GLAZE

2 tbsp (30 ml) ketchup

2 tbsp (30 ml) BBQ sauce

FOR SERVING

Gravy (page 226), optional

Mashed potatoes

Cooked vegetables

Can you believe that you can make something as magnificent as mini meatloaves in 30 minutes? The word *meatloaf* has this connotation that it takes a lot of time and effort to make. It sounds complicated and hard. But in reality, you just combine everything, make a simple two-ingredient glaze, and wait a few minutes for it to cook in the oven. The cooking time is highly reduced in this recipe because, instead of making one big meatloaf, we make four mini meatloaves that taste the same but take way less time to prepare. The result is a tender, juicy mini beef meatloaf with a shiny, sweet glaze. Serve it for special occasions, date night, or a midweek family dinner with some mashed potatoes and cooked vegetables.

Arrange racks in the middle and at the top of the oven, and preheat it to 450°F (230°C). Grease a baking sheet.

For the meatloaf, put the bread in a small bowl and pour the milk over it. Soak the bread for 5 minutes.

In a large bowl, place the beef, shallot, parsley, Worcestershire, garlic powder, egg yolk, and soaked bread. Season the mixture with salt and pepper, and stir it well to combine the ingredients. If the mixture is hard to handle and shape, stir in the panko.

Divide the mixture into four equal portions, then shape each one into a small loaf. Place the loaves on the prepared baking sheet. Drizzle the meatloaves with the olive oil.

Roast the meatloaves on the middle rack of the oven for 15 to 20 minutes, or until a thermometer inserted into the center of each meatloaf registers 160°F (71°C).

Prepare the glaze while the meatloaves are roasting. In a bowl, stir to combine the ketchup and BBQ sauce.

When the meatloaves have reached 160°F (71°C), remove them from the oven, and change the oven temperature to high broil. Brush the loaves with the glaze. Place the baking sheet back in the oven, on the top rack, and broil the loaves for 5 minutes, or until they are golden brown.

To serve, remove the meatloaves from the oven, divide them among four plates, and top them with the gravy, if using. Serve them with the mashed potatoes and vegetables.

LAMB ROAST
with Lentil Salad

SERVES 4

PREP TIME: 5 minutes

ROASTING TIME:
25–30 minutes

If we were to roast the whole leg of lamb, it would take a long time; however, by choosing a smaller piece of meat, we not only reduce the time exponentially, but we get the same result. This super-juicy and incredibly delicious lamb roast can be easily served for holidays and celebrations, but it's also perfect for a very quickly prepared midweek or weekend dinner. The simple lentil and summer vegetable salad balances the lamb beautifully while still making it the main attraction.

LAMB ROAST

2 (1–1½-lb [450–680-g]) top round lamb roasts

Salt and freshly ground black pepper

1 tbsp (15 ml) olive oil

LENTIL SALAD

2 (14-oz [400-g]) cans cooked lentils, drained and rinsed under cold running water

2 tomatoes, cut into small cubes

1 cucumber, peeled and cut into small cubes

1 red onion, chopped

1 cup (160 g) sweet corn kernels

1 spring onion, chopped

2 tbsp (30 ml) olive oil

Salt and freshly ground black pepper

1 tbsp (5 g) ground sumac

1 tbsp (15 ml) freshly squeezed lemon juice

Arrange a rack in the middle of the oven, then preheat it to 450°F (230°C).

For the lamb, season the roasts with salt and pepper. Place the meat in a deep baking dish, and drizzle it with the olive oil.

Place the pan on the middle rack of the oven. Roast the lamb for 25 to 30 minutes, or until a thermometer inserted into the thickest part of the meat registers 135°F (57°C).

Make the lentil salad while the lamb is roasting. In a large bowl, combine the lentils, tomatoes, cucumber, red onion, corn, and spring onion. Drizzle the mixture with the olive oil, and season it with salt and pepper. Add the sumac and lemon juice. Stir to combine all of the ingredients, and set aside the salad.

Remove the lamb roast from the oven, and set it aside to rest for 5 minutes. Cut the lamb into ½-inch (1-cm)-thick slices. Divide the lentil salad among four plates. Place the lamb on top of the salad and serve.

MOROCCAN-SPICED STUFFED LAMB

SERVES 4

PREP TIME: 10 minutes

ROASTING TIME:
20–25 minutes

STUFFED LAMB

3 prunes, chopped

3 dried apricots, chopped

2 slices bread, cut into small cubes

1 tbsp (6 g) panko breadcrumbs

¼ tsp ground cinnamon

¼ tsp ground allspice

1 tbsp (9 g) chopped golden raisins

1 clove garlic, minced

3 tbsp (45 ml) water

2 tbsp (30 ml) olive oil, divided

1 tbsp (5 g) chopped fresh parsley

1 tsp freshly squeezed lemon juice

Salt and freshly ground black pepper

2 (10½–14-oz [300–400-g]) lamb round roasts or rump roasts

FOR SERVING

Squash, Kale, and Israeli Couscous Salad with Cranberries (page 149)

Bring Moroccan flavors to your dining table by making this easy stuffed lamb. It might sound fancy and complicated, but in reality, making stuffed lamb at home is easy, with zero fancy or hardly accessible ingredients. The lamb is succulent and tasty, with a slightly sweet and aromatic stuffing that also serves as a mini side dish. Serve for weeknight dinners, date nights, or holidays, along with a side of a delicious Squash, Kale, and Israeli Couscous Salad with Cranberries (page 149) or, simply, cooked couscous.

Arrange a rack in the middle of the oven, then preheat it to 450°F (230°C). Line a baking sheet with parchment paper.

For the stuffed lamb, in a bowl, combine the prunes, apricots, bread, panko, cinnamon, allspice, raisins, garlic, water, 1 tablespoon (15 ml) of the olive oil, the parsley, and the lemon juice. Season the mixture with salt and pepper.

Using a sharp knife, cut a deep slit into each lamb round to make a pocket. Fill the pockets with the stuffing. Using kitchen string, tie the lamb tightly in three places. Drizzle the stuffed lamb with the remaining 1 tablespoon (15 ml) of olive oil, and season the roast with salt and pepper. Rub the mixture into the meat.

Place the stuffed lamb on the prepared baking sheet. Roast the lamb on the middle rack of the oven for 20 to 25 minutes, or until a thermometer inserted into the thickest part of the meat registers 135°F (57°C). Remove the roast from the oven, and set it aside to rest for a few minutes.

To serve, cut each of the lamb roasts into four slices, and serve with the couscous salad.

RACK OF LAMB
with Mediterranean Herbs

SERVES 4

PREP TIME: 10 minutes

ROASTING TIME:
18–20 minutes

1 clove garlic, finely diced

2 sprigs fresh rosemary, chopped

1 tbsp (5 g) chopped fresh mint

¼ cup (20 g) chopped fresh parsley

1 tbsp (15 ml) plus 2 tsp (10 ml) olive oil, divided

1 tsp sherry vinegar

Salt and freshly ground black pepper

4 (12-oz [350-g]) racks of lamb

Here in Slovenia and in neighboring Italy and Croatia, we are blessed with high-quality, grass-fed lamb meat that is so delicious that it really doesn't need much. Some Mediterranean herbs, salt and pepper, and good-quality olive oil bring out the best from the roasted, tender meat. For the best juiciness and flavor of the meat, it is essential that we don't overcook it. Serve the lamb with Crispy Roasted Potatoes (page 171) or cooked couscous, with a side of Roasted Peppers (page 182) or steamed spring vegetables.

Arrange a rack in the middle of the oven, then preheat it to 430°F (220°C).

In a bowl, combine the garlic, rosemary, mint, parsley, 1 tablespoon (15 ml) of the oil, and vinegar. Season the marinade with salt and pepper. Set it aside until it's needed.

Place a large skillet over medium-high heat. Add 1 teaspoon of the oil. Season the lamb with salt and pepper on both sides. Place two racks of lamb in the hot pan, bone side up, then sear the meat on both sides, 2 minutes per side. Repeat the process with the other teaspoon of oil and two racks of lamb.

Transfer the racks to a deep baking dish. Spoon 2 tablespoons (30 ml) of the herb marinade over the racks, and massage the marinade into the meat. Roast the meat on the middle rack of the oven for 18 to 20 minutes, or until the internal temperature of the thickest part of the meat registers 135°F (57°C).

Remove the dish from the oven, and let the meat rest for 5 minutes. Cut the racks into cutlets, and divide them among four plates. Spoon the remaining marinade over the meat and serve.

LONDON BROIL BEEF STEAK

SERVES 4

PREP TIME: 10 minutes

ROASTING TIME: 14–16 minutes

BEEF

1½ lbs (680 g) top round or flank beef steak

1 tbsp (15 ml) balsamic vinegar

1 tbsp (15 ml) freshly squeezed lemon juice

1 tbsp (15 ml) olive oil, plus more for drizzling

2 cloves garlic, diced

1 sprig fresh rosemary

Salt and freshly ground black pepper

FOR SERVING

Olive oil, optional

Fleur de sel, optional

Crispy Roasted Potatoes (page 171)

Roasted Root Vegetables (page 168)

Grilled bread

London broil beef steak is a tough piece of meat that is first marinated and then broiled or roasted on a high temperature for a short time. That results in a tender, succulent, juicy beef steak that is beautifully seared and crispy on the outside, without using a pricey cut of beef. With this technique, we transform a less fancy cut of meat into a glorious, luxurious weeknight dinner. Serve with potatoes, root vegetables, and a side of grilled bread to absorb the juices.

Arrange a rack at the top of the oven, then preheat it to high broil. Place an ovenproof cast-iron skillet on the top rack of the oven for 10 to 15 minutes to preheat it.

Meanwhile, prepare the steak. Place the beef in a resealable plastic bag, along with the vinegar, lemon juice, oil, garlic, and rosemary. Season the mixture generously with salt and pepper. Close the bag, and massage the mixture into the steak. Set the bag aside for 10 minutes (see Note).

Remove the steak from the marinade, and pat it dry using paper towels. Drizzle the steak with olive oil on both sides.

Using kitchen gloves, carefully remove the cast-iron skillet from the oven.

Place the steak in the hot skillet, and put the pan on the top rack of the oven. Broil the steak for 7 to 8 minutes. Turn the steak, and broil it for another 6 to 7 minutes.

Before removing the steak from the oven, check the temperature. Insert a thermometer into the thickest part of the meat. For rare, the thermometer should register 125°F (52°C); for medium-rare, it should be 130°F (54°C); for medium, it should read 140°F (60°C); and for well-done, 155°F (68°C).

Remove the steak from the oven, and cut it against the grain into thin slices.

To serve, drizzle the steak with oil and sprinkle it with fleur de sel, if using. Serve the meat with the potatoes, root vegetables, and grilled bread.

NOTE: Feel free to marinate the steak up to 24 hours ahead of time. Refrigerate the steak while it's marinating. Remove the steak from the fridge 30 minutes before cooking it.

GINGER, GARLIC, AND SOY STEAK

SERVES 4

PREP TIME: 10 minutes

ROASTING TIME:
6–7 minutes

Mmm, the aroma wafting through the house when searing and roasting this steak is unbelievable. It is so hard waiting for the steak to roast, even though it takes only a few minutes. But, believe me, it is worth the wait because this steak is so incredibly flavorful. The ginger-and-garlic-infused steak is aromatic and sweet, while the texture is soft, tender, and juicy, especially if it is sliced thinly. As sides, serve basmati rice and steamed vegetables.

STEAK

2 (1½-inch [3-cm]-thick) boneless NY strip or top sirloin beef steaks

¼ cup (60 ml) light soy sauce

2 tbsp (30 ml) freshly squeezed lemon juice

2 tbsp (30 ml) honey

Salt and freshly ground black pepper

2 tbsp (30 ml) canola oil

2 cloves garlic, sliced

2-inch (4-cm) piece ginger, thinly sliced

FOR SERVING

Sliced green onions

Sesame seeds

Arrange a rack in the middle of the oven, then preheat it to 450°F (230°C).

For the steak, place the beef in a bowl, along with the soy sauce, lemon juice, and honey. Season the mixture with salt and pepper. Rub the mixture into the meat, and set it aside for 5 minutes. Remove the meat from the marinade, then pat it dry using paper towels. Set aside the marinade to use for the sauce.

Place an ovenproof pan over high heat. When the pan is hot, add the oil and beef to the pan. Lower the heat to medium-high. Sear the steaks on both sides, 1 to 2 minutes per side, moving them around from time to time.

Transfer the pan to the middle rack of the oven. Roast the steak for 6 to 7 minutes. Before removing it from the oven, check the temperature of the steak. Insert a thermometer into the thickest part of the meat. For rare, the thermometer should register 125°F (52°C); for medium-rare, it should be 130°F (54°C); for medium, it should read 140°F (60°C); and for well-done, 155°F (68°C).

Remove the beef from the oven, remove it from the pan, and set it aside to rest for 5 minutes. Place the pan, with the roasting juices, over medium-low heat. Be careful; the pan is very hot. Use protective kitchen gloves. Add the garlic, ginger, and the reserved marinade. Bring the mixture to a boil, then remove it from the heat.

To serve, slice the steak, top it with the sauce, and sprinkle it with the green onions and sesame seeds.

SUPER THIN SANDWICH-STYLE BEEF

SERVES 4

PREP TIME: 10 minutes

ROASTING TIME:
20–25 minutes

BEEF

2–2½ lbs (900 g–1.1 kg) beef eye of round roast or rump steak roast, trimmed and cut into 2 steaks

Salt and freshly ground black pepper

2 tbsp (30 ml) canola oil, divided

2 carrots, chopped

1 onion, chopped

¾ cup (180 ml) beef stock or water

1 bay leaf

FOR SERVING

Sandwich bread

Mustard

Mayonnaise

Gherkins

Fresh lettuce

Sweet Potato Fries (page 167)

This is a recipe inspired by a trip to New York. We visited the famous Katz deli, and, like most people, we were impressed by their classic deli sandwich. We can't make a deli-style beef in 30 minutes, but this is the closest it gets. This beef is succulent, extremely thinly sliced, and so delicious. We prefer roasting it until medium-rare, but feel free to cook it to your taste. Serve the meat stacked between two slices of your favorite bread, along with some condiments. For some extra flavor, soak one side of the bread in the roasting juices.

Arrange a rack in the middle of the oven, then preheat it to 480°F (250°C). Place a Dutch oven pot on the stove to preheat over high heat.

For the beef, season each piece of meat with salt and pepper. Drizzle the beef with 1 tablespoon (15 ml) of the oil, and rub the mixture into the meat.

Put the remaining 1 tablespoon (15 ml) of oil in the Dutch oven. When the oil gets hot, add the beef, and sear the meat on all sides, 2 minutes per side. Remove the beef from the pot. Add the carrots, onion, stock, and bay leaf to the pot, and place the beef on top of the vegetables, above the liquid.

Transfer the pan to the middle rack of the oven. Roast the meat for 15 minutes; turn the meat twice while roasting. Then, cover the pot with a lid. Reduce the oven temperature to 430°F (220°C), and roast the meat for another 5 to 10 minutes, or until a thermometer inserted into the thickest part of the meat registers 125°F (52°C).

Remove the beef from the oven, and let it rest, covered, for 5 to 10 minutes.

For serving, slice the beef against the grain as thinly as possible. Make sandwiches with the beef, sandwich bread, mustard, mayonnaise, gherkins, and lettuce. Serve the sweet potato fries on the side.

VENISON LOIN
with a Creamy Sauce

SERVES 4

PREP TIME: 10 minutes

ROASTING TIME:
6–8 minutes

VENISON
2 (1-lb [450-g]) venison loins, trimmed

Salt and freshly ground black pepper

1 tbsp (15 ml) canola oil

4 tbsp (56 g) unsalted butter

4 cloves garlic, smashed

CREAMY SAUCE
2 shallots, finely diced

½ cup (120 ml) sweet white wine or brandy

½ cup (120 ml) heavy cream

⅔ cup (160 ml) beef stock

2 tbsp (10 g) chopped fresh parsley or chives

FOR SERVING
Crispy Roasted Potatoes (page 171)

Cooked green beans

Venison has a particular gamy, intense flavor, so it is good to pair it with something light, sweet, and complementary in flavor. For this recipe, we first sear the meat in a skillet, then finish it in the oven. While the venison is resting, make the sauce, using the full-of-flavor roasting juices, wine or a good-quality brandy, heavy cream, and some parsley for freshness. This easily prepared dinner tastes great and is fancy enough for celebrations and date night.

Arrange a rack in the middle of the oven, then preheat it to 410°F (210°C).

For the venison, season the meat with salt and pepper. Drizzle the meat with the oil, and rub the mixture into the meat.

Place an ovenproof cast-iron skillet over high heat. When it is smoking hot, add the venison, and sear it on all sides, 1 to 2 minutes per side. Then, add the butter and garlic to the skillet, and transfer it to the oven. Roast the meat on the middle rack for 6 to 8 minutes. Before removing it from the oven, check the temperature of the venison. Insert a thermometer into the thickest part of the meat. For rare, the thermometer should register 125°F (52°C); for medium-rare, it should be 130°F (54°C); for medium, it should read 140°F (60°C); and for well-done, 155°F (68°C).

Remove the venison from the oven, and transfer it to a plate to rest.

While the venison is resting, make the sauce. Remove most of the butter from the roasting skillet—be careful, the skillet is scorching hot—but leave the roasting juices. Place the skillet over medium-high heat. Add the shallots, cook for 1 minute, then add the wine. Cook for 2 to 3 minutes, to allow the alcohol to evaporate. Add the cream and stock, bring the mixture to a boil, and cook it for 2 to 3 minutes. Remove the pan from the stove; stir in the parsley.

For serving, slice the venison, divide it among four plates, and pour the sauce over it. Serve the meat with the potatoes and green beans.

SOFT ITALIAN MEATBALLS

SERVES 4

PREP TIME: 10 minutes

ROASTING TIME:
18–20 minutes

There is nothing more soothing and comforting than a bowl of soft, delicious, warm meatballs with homemade tomato sauce and mashed potatoes or spaghetti. These two-bite–sized meatballs are made with ground beef chuck, which has enough fat to make them juicy and flavorful. This foolproof recipe will feed the whole family, and you can easily make them ahead of time. Freeze shaped meatballs in freezer bags, and then cook them on a hectic weeknight—just make sure to roast frozen meatballs for a couple of minutes longer.

MEATBALLS

2 thick slices stale bread, crusts removed and bread cut into small cubes

⅓ cup (80 ml) warm milk

1 lb (450 g) ground beef chuck

½ onion, minced

1 clove garlic, minced

1 tbsp (5 g) chopped fresh parsley

⅓ cup (33 g) freshly grated Parmesan cheese

Salt and freshly ground black pepper

½ tsp dried oregano

¼ tsp freshly grated nutmeg

1 egg

1 tbsp (15 ml) olive oil, plus more for drizzling

2 tbsp (29 g) mascarpone, ricotta, or cream cheese

TOMATO SAUCE

1 tbsp (15 ml) olive oil

½ onion, diced

1 clove garlic, diced

1 tbsp (9 g) all-purpose flour

1 tsp sugar

17 oz (480 g) canned diced tomatoes, with liquid

½ cup (120 ml) water

½ tsp dried oregano

Salt and freshly ground black pepper

1 tbsp (5 g) chopped fresh basil or parsley

FOR SERVING

Freshly grated Parmesan cheese, optional

Cooked spaghetti or mashed potatoes

Arrange a rack in the middle of the oven, then preheat it to 450°F (230°C). Grease a baking sheet.

For the meatballs, put the bread in a bowl, pour the milk over it, and set aside the mixture to soak.

Put the meat in a large bowl, along with the onion, garlic, parsley, and Parmesan. Season with salt and pepper; add the oregano and nutmeg. Add the soaked bread, egg, oil, and mascarpone cheese to the meat mixture. Stir well to combine everything.

Divide the mixture into twelve parts. Using wet hands, roll each piece into a meatball. Place the meatballs on a baking sheet. Drizzle the meatballs with olive oil, and place the baking sheet in the oven, on the middle rack. Roast the meatballs for 18 to 20 minutes, or until they are browned and cooked through.

While the meatballs are roasting, make the sauce. Heat the oil in a medium-sized saucepan over medium-high heat. Add the onion and garlic, stir, and cook them for 1 minute. Add the flour and sugar, mix well, and cook for 2 to 3 minutes. Then add the tomatoes, water, and oregano. Bring the mixture to a boil, season it with salt and pepper, and cook it for 5 minutes. Sprinkle the basil on top.

To serve, top the roasted Italian meatballs with the tomato sauce and Parmesan, if using, and serve with the spaghetti.

TENDERLOIN STEAKS
with Creamy Peppercorn Sauce

SERVES 4

PREP TIME: 10 minutes

ROASTING TIME: 8 minutes

TENDERLOIN

4 (8-oz [220-g]) beef tenderloin steaks
or filet mignon

Salt and freshly ground black pepper

1 tbsp (15 ml) canola oil

PEPPERCORN SAUCE

1 shallot, finely diced

1 clove garlic, crushed

2 tbsp (28 g) unsalted butter

1 tsp Dijon mustard

¼ cup (60 ml) brandy or cognac

½ cup (120 ml) beef stock

½ cup (120 ml) heavy cream

1 tbsp (15 g) green peppercorns

½ tsp Worcestershire or Maggi sauce

FOR SERVING

Crispy Roasted Potatoes (page 171)

Chicory Salad with Golden Raisins
(page 158)

These steaks with a super-creamy peppercorn sauce are our all-time favorite. The juicy, tender, lip-smacking steaks are covered in a sweet, luscious peppercorn sauce made from beef stock, shallots, brandy, heavy cream, and, of course, peppercorns. They are perfect for celebrations, holidays, or a special date-night dinner when you really want to impress your loved one. It takes less than twenty minutes to prepare the steaks, but they taste just as they would in a super-fancy restaurant.

Arrange a rack in the middle of the oven, then preheat it to 410°F (210°C).

For the tenderloins, place a skillet over medium-high heat. Pat the meat dry, and season it with salt and pepper on both sides. When the skillet is smoking hot, add the oil and the steaks. Sear on all sides, 1 to 2 minutes per side.

Transfer the seared steaks to a baking sheet. Roast the steaks on the middle rack of the oven for 6 to 8 minutes. Before removing the steaks from the oven, check the temperature of the meat. Insert a thermometer into the thickest part of the meat. For rare, the thermometer should register 125°F (52°C); for medium-rare, it should be 130°F (54°C); for medium, it should read 140°F (60°C); and for well-done, 155°F (68°C).

While the steaks are roasting, make the sauce. Place the skillet back over low heat. Add the shallot, garlic, butter, and Dijon. Stir and cook for 2 to 3 minutes. Add the brandy, cook for 1 minute, then add the beef stock, and bring the mixture to a boil. Pour in the cream, stir to combine, and cook the sauce for 3 to 5 minutes to thicken it. Then add the peppercorns and Worcestershire sauce. Stir them in, and remove the sauce from the heat.

To serve, divide the steaks among four plates, pour the peppercorn sauce over the steaks, and serve them with the roasted potatoes and salad.

OVEN-GRILLED FLANKEN-STYLE BEEF SHORT RIBS

SERVES 4

PREP TIME: 10 minutes

ROASTING TIME: 5 minutes

SHORT RIBS

1½ lbs (680 g) flanken-style beef short ribs

1 tbsp (5 g) smoked paprika

1 tsp garlic powder

1 tsp ground coriander

1 tsp cumin

Salt and freshly ground black pepper

2 tbsp (30 ml) olive oil

1 tbsp (15 ml) vegetable oil

FOR SERVING

Pickled vegetables (see Note)

Grilled bread

Chopped fresh cilantro, optional

Lime wedges, optional

If we asked you to try this dish with your eyes closed and guess where it was cooked, you would have never guessed that it was not made on an outdoor grill. This dish has that charred flavor that is so specific to grilling—flavorful, rich, and smoky. Oh gosh, and these are so juicy, tender, and tasty. For a maximum flavor explosion in your mouth, serve them with homemade or store-bought pickled vegetables and grilled bread or Crispy Roasted Potatoes (page 171). This is an easy weeknight or weekend dinner for all seasons.

Arrange a rack at the top of the oven, then preheat it to high broil.

For the short ribs, place the ribs on a plate. Season them on both sides with the paprika, garlic powder, coriander, cumin, salt, and pepper, then drizzle them with the olive oil. Rub the mixture into the meat.

Place an ovenproof skillet over medium-high heat. When the pan is hot, add the vegetable oil and short ribs to the skillet. Cook for 1 minute, turn the ribs over, and place the pan on the top rack in the oven. Broil for 3 to 5 minutes, or until the ribs are crisp and browned. Remove the pan from the oven, and let the meat rest for 5 minutes.

To serve, plate the ribs alongside the pickled vegetables and grilled bread. Sprinkle the ribs with the cilantro and serve them with lime wedges, if using.

NOTE: Making homemade pickled vegetables is so easy. Thinly slice radishes, onions, or cucumbers using a mandoline slicer or a small sharp knife. In a small bowl, combine ½ cup (120 ml) of white wine vinegar, ½ cup (120 ml) of water, 1 tablespoon (15 g) of sugar, and a pinch of salt. Stir well to dissolve the sugar. Add the sliced vegetables, let them sit for 10 minutes, then serve.

OVEN-ROASTED T-BONE STEAK
with Herb Butter

SERVES 2

PREP TIME: 10 minutes

ROASTING TIME:
2–12 minutes

HERB BUTTER

½ cup (115 g) unsalted butter, softened

1 clove garlic, minced

2 tbsp (10 g) chopped fresh mixed herbs, such as cilantro, parsley, or tarragon

1 tsp finely diced capers

Salt and freshly ground black pepper

STEAK

1–1½ lbs (450–680 g) T-bone steak

Salt and freshly ground black pepper

2 tbsp (30 ml) olive oil, divided

1 tbsp (14 g) unsalted butter

2 cloves garlic, crushed

1 sprig fresh rosemary

FOR SERVING

Green Bean Salad with Mustard Dressing (page 150)

Grilled bread

Forget about needing to go to a fancy restaurant to have a delicious piece of T-bone steak. This steak is perfect for all meat lovers. Juicy, tender meat is topped with melting herb butter, which gives the steak so much flavor and aroma. Use a cast-iron skillet for this recipe because it will be so easy to sear the steak on the stove and then transfer it to the oven to finish. We love to broil this steak to medium-rare or medium because the steak will be full of those delicious juices, and the meat will be soft and cooked to perfection. However, if you prefer your steak well-done, you can achieve it in 12 minutes. After leaving the steak to rest for a couple of minutes, serve it with the homemade herb butter and sides.

Arrange a rack at the top of the oven, then preheat it to high broil.

For the herb butter, put the butter in a bowl, along with the garlic, herbs, and capers. Season the mixture generously with salt and pepper. Use an electric mixer to combine everything and make a creamy herb butter. Set aside the mixture.

For the steak, arrange a wire rack over a baking sheet, and set it aside.

Place a large, ovenproof cast-iron skillet over high heat for 2 minutes, or until it's smoking hot. Pat the steak dry using paper towels. Season the steak with salt and pepper. Drizzle it with 1 tablespoon (15 ml) of the oil. Put the remaining 1 tablespoon (15 ml) of oil in the hot skillet. Add the steak, and sear it on one side for 2 to 3 minutes. Flip the steak, then put the unsalted butter on top of the steak. Add the garlic and rosemary, and transfer the steak to the oven, on the top rack.

Broil the steak for 2 to 4 minutes, or until a thermometer inserted into the thickest part of the meat registers 125°F (52°C) for rare. Broil for 4 to 6 minutes, or to a temperature of 130°F (54°C), for medium-rare. Broil for 6 to 8 minutes, or to 140°F (60°C), for medium, or 8 to 12 minutes, or to 155°F (68°C), for well-done. Remove the steak from the oven and transfer it to the prepared wire rack. Pour the remaining roasting juices over the steak, and let it rest for 5 minutes.

To serve, cut the steak into the desired thickness of slices, top the slices with dollops of herb butter, and serve them with the salad and bread.

TURKISH BEEF KÖFTAS

SERVES 4

PREP TIME: 10 minutes

ROASTING TIME:
14–16 minutes

KÖFTAS

1 lb (450 g) ground beef

2 tbsp (12 g) panko breadcrumbs

2 cloves garlic, minced

½ onion, minced

¼ cup (60 ml) water

1 tsp baking powder

½ tsp ground sumac

1 tsp paprika

1 tsp dried mint

¼ tsp ground cumin

2 tbsp (10 g) chopped fresh parsley

Salt and freshly ground black pepper

FOR SERVING

Pita bread

Yogurt

Fresh vegetables, such as cabbage, tomatoes, and cucumber

Turkish Roasted Red Pepper Dip (page 235)

These easy and quick-to-make beef kebabs are known as köftas. They are a delicious midweek dinner for any day of the year, for all seasons. The spices in these ground beef köftas are easily accessible, and they will create Turkish flavors in the comfort of your own home. The köftas are slightly charred and just as delicious as they would be if you prepared them on the outside grill. Serve them with pita bread, yogurt, and fresh vegetables, or keep the meal light and simply serve them with a seasonal salad.

Arrange a rack at the top of the oven, then preheat it to 450°F (230°C). If you are using wooden skewers, cover them with water in a shallow pan to soak them for 10 minutes.

For the köftas, in a bowl, combine the beef, panko, garlic, onion, water, baking powder, sumac, paprika, mint, cumin, and parsley. Season the mixture with salt and pepper, and knead it with your hands.

Divide the mixture into eight parts and, using slightly wet hands, mold them onto metal or wooden skewers. Leave a few inches from the skewers' handles and tips.

Line up the skewers on a baking sheet, and place it on the top rack of the oven. Roast the kebabs for 10 to 12 minutes. Then, set the oven to low broil. Broil the köftas for 4 minutes, or until they are brown and slightly charred.

To serve, remove the köftas from the oven, and serve them with the pita bread, yogurt, vegetables, and Turkish Roasted Red Pepper Dip on the side.

JUICY POULTRY FOR ANY OCCASION

Chicken and other poultry, such as turkey and duck, are the best types of meat to roast if you are in a hurry or if you want to prepare a stress-free dinner during a busy week. Both the white and dark parts of the meat are perfect for roasting since they don't take a lot of time to cook. All the recipes in this book have been tested and modified so that you can easily make them in 30 minutes or less, while keeping the tasty juiciness and tenderness of the meat.

There are some classic recipes in this book, like our all-time favorite roasted chicken. For the perfect recipe Crispy Roasted Chicken Halves (page 48), we cut the chicken in half instead of roasting it whole. That simple trick reduces the cooking time significantly without losing any of the flavor, texture, and deliciousness. Roasted Chicken Thighs with Grapes and Polenta (page 52) will transport you to the sunny Mediterranean. Delicious chicken thighs, sweet, juicy roasted grapes, and incredibly creamy polenta—such a delightful summer or autumn dish. Then, we have our favorite weeknight dinner, Sweet and Sour Roasted Turkey Meatballs (page 60). The tastiest little turkey meatballs result from just 15 minutes of oven roasting. Not only are they super flavorful and rich, but they can easily be prepared in advance, and they freeze beautifully, too.

If you are learning how to cook and want to learn how to extract the most flavor out of each ingredient, roasting is a great way to go. Also, poultry is inexpensive and easy to prepare, and it doesn't take a lot of time out of your busy schedule. We are sure you will love these easy recipes, whether you are a beginner or an advanced cook.

CRISPY ROASTED CHICKEN HALVES

SERVES 4

PREP TIME: 5 minutes

ROASTING TIME:
25–30 minutes

CHICKEN

1 (2–3-lb [1–1⅓-kg]) whole chicken

2 tbsp (30 ml) canola oil

Salt and freshly ground black pepper

FOR SERVING

Crispy Roasted Potatoes (page 171)

Roasted Root Vegetables (page 168)

Sure, it seems impossible to roast a whole chicken in 30 minutes. But we can use some tricks, such as cutting the chicken, to make it work. Roasted chicken is the most magnificent meal that can be served for all holidays, celebrations, or weekend family dinners. In our family, it is always on the menu for Christmas, and it often takes a lot of time and preparation. However, juicy and tender roasted chicken shouldn't be reserved for special occasions only. That's why we came up with a quick and simple way to cook it in just 30 minutes, without any overpowering spices and herbs. Just plain and simple, a succulent, tender chicken with a delicious, crispy skin.

Arrange a rack in the middle of the oven, then preheat it to 480°F (250°C). Place a wire rack on a baking sheet.

For the chicken, place the chicken, breast side down with the wings facing toward you, on a work surface. Use a sharp knife or poultry shears to cut down both sides of the backbone, then remove it. Cut closely to the spine so that you do not remove too much meat. Open the rib cage, and use a heavy chef's knife to cut through the breast bone. Split the chicken lengthwise down the center to make two halves. Now, cut each drumstick at the thickest part until you hit a bone.

Pat the chicken halves dry using paper towels. Brush the oil over the chicken halves, then generously season them on both sides with salt and pepper. Place the chicken, skin side up, on the prepared wire rack.

Roast the chicken on the middle rack of the oven for 20 minutes. Then reduce the temperature to 450°F (230°C). Roast the chicken for 5 to 10 minutes, or until it's just golden brown or a thermometer inserted into the thickest part of the meat registers 160°F (71°C).

Allow the chicken to rest, covered, for at least 3 to 4 minutes before carving it.

Serve the chicken with the potatoes and root vegetables.

DATE-NIGHT CORNISH HENS FOR TWO

SERVES 2

PREP TIME: 5 minutes

ROASTING TIME: 25–30 minutes

CORNISH HENS

2 (1½-lb [680-g]) Cornish game hens

Salt and freshly ground black pepper

2 tbsp (30 ml) canola oil

2 lemon wedges

2 cloves garlic, peeled and smashed

2 sprigs fresh thyme

FOR SERVING

Gravy (page 226) or Béarnaise Sauce (page 230)

These crispy yet juicy and tender hens are the perfect dinner for a special date night. Whether you want to celebrate an anniversary, an exceptional achievement, a birthday, Valentine's Day, or you just want to surprise your loved one with a spectacular and delicious meal, this is the recipe for you. Cornish hens are very small chickens, perfect for two people, but we prepare one for each person so we have leftovers for salad or a sandwich the next day. These hens roast quickly, while still achieving that crispy, golden-brown roasted skin we all love. Serve this with Crispy Roasted Potatoes (page 171) and Green Bean Salad with Mustard Dressing (page 150).

Arrange a rack in the middle of the oven, then preheat it to 480°F (250°C). Place a wire rack on a baking sheet.

For the Cornish hens, pat the chickens dry using paper towels. Season them with salt and pepper, and brush them with the oil. Place a lemon wedge, a clove of garlic, and a sprig of thyme into the cavity of each hen. Place the hens on the prepared wire rack.

Roast the hens on the middle rack of the oven for 20 minutes. Then, reduce the temperature to 450°F (230°C), and roast the hens for 5 to 10 minutes, or until just golden brown. Before removing the hens from the oven, check the temperature of the chicken. A thermometer inserted into the thickest part of the meat should register 160°F (71°C). Remove the hens from the oven, and let them rest for a few minutes before serving.

To serve, transfer the hens to a serving platter. Remove the meat from the bones, then slice and serve with the gravy.

ROASTED CHICKEN THIGHS

with Grapes and Polenta

SERVES 4

PREP TIME: 5 minutes

ROASTING TIME:
18–20 minutes

CHICKEN THIGHS

2 lbs (900 g) boneless chicken thighs, skin on

Salt and freshly ground black pepper

1 tsp ground mustard

2 tbsp (30 ml) olive oil, divided

4 whole, peeled shallots

¼ cup (60 ml) sherry vinegar

¼ cup (60 ml) Madeira, Marsala, or other sweet wine

2 cups (300 g) seedless red grapes

POLENTA

3 cups (720 ml) water

1 tsp salt

¾ cup (120 g) instant polenta

2 tbsp (28 g) unsalted butter

FOR SERVING

Chopped walnuts, optional

Fresh oregano leaves, optional

Olive oil, optional

We both grew up surrounded by vineyards, so grapes hold a special place in our hearts. Each year, the vines are full of juicy, sweet, purple grapes, but you can only make so many jams, marmalades, and cakes. Adding grapes to delicious roasted chicken is just the ultimate autumn meal. The sweet aroma of grapes roasting in the oven is one that fills our hearts with happiness and calmness. In this dish, you will discover deliciously roasted and crispy chicken thighs and juicy, fruity grapes, a divine combination of two completely different flavors. Serve the thighs with some creamy polenta, then devour this simple yet incredibly delicious autumn comfort meal.

Preheat the oven to 450°F (230°C).

For the chicken thighs, place a large ovenproof nonstick skillet over high heat until the pan is hot but not smoking. Sprinkle the chicken with salt, pepper, and the mustard, then brush it with 1 tablespoon (15 ml) of the oil. Put the remaining 1 tablespoon (15 ml) of oil in the skillet, add the chicken thighs, skin side down, and pan roast them for 6 to 8 minutes, or until the fat renders and the skin is golden brown. Remove as much fat from the skillet as possible.

Flip the chicken to skin side up, then reduce the heat to medium-high. Add the shallots, vinegar, wine, and grapes. Transfer the skillet to the oven, and roast the chicken for 18 to 20 minutes, or until the chicken is golden brown; a thermometer inserted into the thickest part of the meat should read 165°F (74°C).

Prepare the polenta while the thighs roast. In a saucepan, bring the water to a boil. Add the salt, and gradually whisk in the polenta. Cook the polenta over low heat, continually stirring, until it's thick and it pulls away from the side of the pan, for 8 to 10 minutes. Remove the pan from the heat, stir in the butter, and cover the pan to keep the polenta warm. The polenta will stay warm, covered, for 10 to 15 minutes. Stir the polenta just before serving it.

To serve, remove the chicken from the oven. Divide it and the polenta among four plates. Sprinkle the plates with the walnuts and oregano leaves, if using. Drizzle olive oil over the chicken, if using.

TURKEY BREAST ROULADE
with Prunes

This recipe is magnificent enough to make for celebrations, Thanksgiving dinner, or a quick midweek dinner. We stuff sweet prunes into juicy turkey breast. To get it roasted and on the table in 30 minutes, we need to use some tricks. First, we pound the turkey with the rolling pin (or a meat tenderizer) to get a thinner breast. Then, we cut it in half to make two smaller roulades, which then roast for less than the target 30 minutes. This simple yet fancy dinner is even better when served with mashed potatoes and roasted rutabagas.

SERVES 4

PREP TIME: 7 minutes

ROASTING TIME: 23–25 minutes

ROULADES

1½–2 lbs (680–900 g) boneless turkey breast, butterflied

Salt and freshly ground black pepper

¾ cup (120 g) chopped prunes

1 tbsp (15 ml) canola oil

FOR SERVING

Gravy (page 226)

Maple Syrup–Glazed Rutabaga with Pancetta (page 157)

Mashed potatoes

Arrange a rack in the middle of the oven, then preheat it to 480°F (250°C). Line a baking sheet with parchment paper.

For the roulades, season the turkey with salt and pepper on both sides. Using a rolling pin, pound the breast until it is ½ inch (1 cm) thick. Then, cut the breast in half, and spread the chopped prunes over the middle of each halved turkey breast. Roll each breast half into a small roll. Tie each roulade with kitchen string every 1 inch (2 cm), so it holds its shape.

Transfer the roulades to the prepared baking sheet, and brush them with the canola oil.

Roast the roulades on the middle rack of the oven for 15 minutes. Then reduce the heat to 450°F (230°C). Roast the roulades for 8 to 10 minutes. Before removing the roulades from the oven, check the temperature of the turkey. A thermometer inserted into the thickest part of the meat should register 160°F (71°C).

Remove the roulades from the oven, and let the turkey rest for a few minutes before serving.

To serve, slice the roulades and serve them with the gravy, rutabaga, and potatoes.

CHICKEN LEGS
with Root Vegetables

SERVES 4

PREP TIME: 5 minutes

ROASTING TIME:
25 minutes

CHICKEN LEGS

2 orange carrots, halved lengthwise

2 yellow carrots, halved lengthwise

1 cup (150 g) 1-inch (2-cm) cubes of rutabaga

1 cup (150 g) 1-inch (2-cm) cubes of celery root

4 (½-lb [225-g]) chicken legs, cut at the knee joint to separate the thigh from the drumstick

Salt and freshly ground black pepper

½ tsp dried thyme

2 tbsp (30 ml) olive oil

FOR SERVING

Chopped fresh parsley, optional

Gravy (page 226)

This sheet-pan dinner will feed the whole family. Perfectly crispy chicken legs are paired with sweet root vegetables that make the perfect side. This chicken roast has all the components a good roast should have. It is perfectly crispy and baked outside, with a juicy, tender interior that is cooked to perfection. Serve it for Sunday dinner or small gatherings, but it is so quick and straightforward that you can easily make it any time of the week. The root vegetables side is sweet and cooked, but not overcooked. However, feel free to make Crispy Roasted Potatoes (page 171) or Sweet Potato Fries (page 167) as an extra side dish.

Arrange racks in the middle and at the top of the oven, then preheat it to 450°F (230°C).

For the chicken legs, arrange the orange and yellow carrots, rutabaga, and celery root on a baking sheet. Place the chicken leg pieces on top of the vegetables. Season the chicken with the salt, pepper, and thyme. Drizzle the pan with the olive oil, and toss the ingredients to coat them with the oil.

Roast the chicken and vegetables on the middle rack of the oven for 15 minutes.

Increase the oven temperature to high broil. Then, move the pan, with kitchen gloves to protect from the heat, to the top rack of the oven. Broil the chicken for 10 minutes, or until a thermometer inserted into the thickest part of the meat registers 160°F (71°C).

To serve, sprinkle the dish with the parsley, if using, and serve the chicken with the gravy.

BREAD-STUFFED CHICKEN BREAST

SERVES 4

PREP TIME: 5 minutes

ROASTING TIME:
20–25 minutes

CHICKEN

4 slices white bread, cut into small cubes

⅓ cup (80 ml) heavy cream

1 tbsp (15 ml) olive oil

½ onion, diced

1 clove garlic, diced

1 tbsp (5 g) chopped fresh parsley

1 egg yolk

¼ tsp freshly grated nutmeg

Salt and freshly ground black pepper

2 (8–10½-oz [220–300-g]) boneless chicken breasts, skin on

FOR SERVING

Mashed potatoes

Roasted Root Vegetables (page 168)

Gravy (page 226)

Bread-stuffed chicken breast is our favorite recipe from Jernej's mom. She would always prepare the stuffing one day ahead and refrigerate the bread mixture overnight to let the flavors meld. Sometimes she added pan-fried bacon to the mixture to add even more flavor to the stuffing. Bread-stuffed chicken breast is one of those dishes that you can easily serve for holidays, gatherings, celebrations, or a special yet easily prepared weeknight dinner. It is incredibly flavorful and rich, and its moist, juicy bread stuffing makes a wonderful side. We serve this with potatoes, vegetables, and a seasonal salad.

Arrange a rack in the middle of the oven, then preheat it to 465°F (240°C). Line a baking sheet with parchment paper.

For the chicken, stir together the bread and cream in a bowl. Add the oil, onion, garlic, parsley, egg yolk, and nutmeg, and stir to combine the ingredients. Season the mixture with salt and pepper.

Season the chicken breasts with salt and pepper on both sides.

Lift the skin off the chicken breasts, and fill each with half of the bread stuffing. Using a kitchen string, tie the chicken breast in two places to close the skin.

Place the stuffed chicken, skin side down, on the prepared baking sheet. Roast the chicken on the middle rack of the oven for 20 to 25 minutes, turning it halfway through the cooking time.

Before removing the chicken from the oven, check the temperature. A thermometer inserted into the thickest part of the meat should register 160°F (71°C).

To serve, cut each stuffed chicken breast in half, and divide the pieces among four plates. Add the potatoes and vegetables to the plates. Top the chicken with the gravy.

SWEET AND SOUR ROASTED TURKEY MEATBALLS

Asian-inspired flavor fills these delicate, soft, light, and lemon-scented meatballs, and the sauce leaves you with that umami flavor that we all love and adore. It is creamy and rich, yet not overpowering. This dish is perfect for a quick and easy weeknight family dinner. It won't take you a lot of time or effort to make. Do expect a lot of praise and rave reviews for this one.

MEATBALLS

1 1/3 lbs (600 g) ground turkey

Salt and freshly ground black pepper

1/2 onion, diced

1 tbsp (5 g) chopped parsley

2 cloves garlic, minced

1 tsp freshly grated ginger

1 tsp diced preserved lemon

1 tbsp (15 ml) light soy sauce

1 medium egg

3 tbsp (18 g) panko breadcrumbs

2 tbsp (30 ml) sesame oil

SWEET AND SOUR STICKY SAUCE

3/4 cup (180 ml) water

1/4 cup (60 g) tomato passata or tomato puree

1 tbsp (15 ml) light soy sauce

1 tbsp (15 ml) oyster sauce

1 tbsp (15 ml) Worcestershire sauce

2 tbsp (30 ml) rice vinegar or apple cider vinegar

1 tbsp (15 g) brown sugar

1 clove garlic, minced

1/2 tsp freshly grated ginger

FOR SERVING

Sesame seeds, optional

Finely chopped spring onion, optional

Cooked basmati rice

Steamed bok choy or broccoli

Arrange racks in the middle and at the top of the oven, then preheat it to 450°F (230°C).

For the meatballs, in a large bowl, combine the turkey, salt, pepper, onion, parsley, garlic, ginger, lemon, soy sauce, egg, and panko. The mixture will be a little bit wet, but that will result in soft, tender meatballs. Divide the mixture into twelve pieces, and, using wet hands, roll the mixture into round meatballs.

Place a large nonstick skillet over high heat. Add the sesame oil and pan-fry the meatballs on both sides, 2 minutes per side. Transfer the meatballs to a deep baking dish. Roast the meatballs on the middle rack of the oven for 10 minutes.

Make the sauce while the meatballs are roasting. In a saucepan, combine the water, passata, soy sauce, oyster sauce, Worcestershire, vinegar, sugar, garlic, and ginger. Place the pan over medium-high heat, bring the mixture to a boil, then cook it for 5 minutes, or until the sauce is reduced by one-third.

Remove the roasted meatballs from the oven, using gloves to protect from the heat. Increase the oven temperature to high broil.

Pour the sauce evenly over the meatballs, and place them on the top rack of the oven. Broil them for 5 minutes, or until the meatballs are caramelized and crispy and the sauce is slightly thickened.

To serve, remove the meatballs from the oven, and sprinkle them with the sesame seeds and onion, if using. Serve the meatballs and sticky sauce over the rice, with the bok choy on the side.

LEMON CHICKEN KEBABS

SERVES 4

PREP TIME: 10 minutes

ROASTING TIME: 20 minutes

These yogurt-and-herb-marinated chicken skewers will soon become your favorite. This Mediterranean-inspired healthy dinner for busy weeknights can be prepared any time of year. The chicken is flavorful, slightly citrusy, aromatic, and juicy. Chicken breasts don't take long to roast, yet there is still enough time in between to make a simple Turkish Roasted Red Pepper Dip (page 235). Serve the kebabs with flatbread, fresh vegetables, such as diced tomatoes and lettuce, and a spoonful of the fantastic homemade dip.

KEBABS

2 (10–12-oz [280–340-g]) boneless, skinless chicken breasts, cut into 1-inch (2-cm) chunks

2 tbsp (30 ml) Greek yogurt

1 tsp freshly grated lemon zest

1 tbsp (15 ml) freshly squeezed lemon juice

1 tbsp (15 ml) olive oil, plus more for drizzling

½ tsp dried oregano

1 tsp paprika

2 cloves garlic, diced

Salt and freshly ground black pepper

FOR SERVING

Pita bread

Fresh vegetables

Tzatziki, optional

Turkish Roasted Red Pepper Dip (page 235)

Arrange a rack at the top of the oven, then preheat it to high broil. Line a baking sheet with parchment paper. If you are using wooden skewers, cover them with water in a shallow pan to soak them for 10 minutes.

For the kebabs, in a large bowl, mix the chicken, yogurt, lemon zest, lemon juice, oil, oregano, paprika, and garlic. Season with salt and pepper, and stir well to combine.

Use four metal or wooden skewers long enough to sit across the prepared baking sheet. Thread the chicken onto the skewers, and put the skewers crosswise on the prepared baking sheet. Drizzle the chicken with the olive oil. Broil the kebabs on the top rack of the oven for 10 minutes, then turn them and broil them for 10 minutes, or until they are cooked and tender inside, while slightly charred and grilled outside.

To serve, plate the kebabs with the pita bread, vegetables, and tzatziki, if using. Spoon some of the red pepper dip over the chicken.

TERIYAKI CHICKEN BREAST

SERVES 4

PREP TIME: 5 minutes

ROASTING TIME: 25 minutes

This Japanese-inspired chicken recipe is absolutely addictive. Juicy, roasted chicken breasts are glazed with a homemade teriyaki sauce, which is made from simple ingredients in just a couple of minutes. This teriyaki chicken will definitely elevate your weeknight menu; it is bursting with flavors and, because the breasts are covered in the sauce, they don't become dry. Serve with basmati rice and steamed vegetables for a quick and healthy midweek dinner.

CHICKEN

2 (10–12-oz [280–340-g]) boneless, skinless chicken breasts

1 tbsp (15 ml) sesame oil

1 tsp light soy sauce

½ tsp ground ginger

¼ tsp garlic powder

Salt and freshly ground black pepper

HOMEMADE TERIYAKI SAUCE

½ cup (120 ml) light soy sauce

¼ cup (60 ml) water

1 clove garlic, minced

1-inch (2-cm) piece ginger, grated

¼ cup (60 ml) freshly squeezed orange juice

⅓ cup (80 ml) honey

1 tsp rice vinegar or apple cider vinegar

FOR SERVING

Cooked basmati rice

Steamed vegetables

Seasame seeds

Sliced green onion

Arrange racks in the middle and at the top of the oven, then preheat it to 465°F (240°C).

For the chicken, season the breasts with the sesame oil, soy sauce, ginger, garlic powder, salt, and pepper. Rub the seasoning into the meat, then transfer the chicken to a sheet pan. Roast the chicken for 20 minutes on the middle rack of the oven.

Make the teriyaki sauce while the chicken is roasting. In a saucepan, combine the soy sauce, water, garlic, ginger, orange juice, honey, and vinegar. Place the pan over high heat and bring the sauce to a boil, then reduce the heat to low and cook for about 10 minutes, or until the sauce is reduced by two-thirds. Using a ladle, remove ¼ cup (60 ml) of the sauce.

Remove the chicken breasts from the oven. Brush the ¼ cup (60 ml) of sauce all over the chicken breasts. Change the oven temperature to high broil. Using gloves to protect from the heat, put the pan on the top rack of the oven, and broil the chicken for 5 minutes, or until a thermometer inserted into the thickest part of the meat registers 160°F (71°C).

Remove the chicken from the oven, slice it, and serve it with a side of teriyaki sauce and the rice and steamed vegetables. Garnish with sesame seeds and green onion.

STICKY BBQ CHICKEN WINGS

SERVES 4

PREP TIME: 5 minutes

ROASTING TIME:
25 minutes

CHICKEN WINGS

1 tsp paprika

½ tsp ground coriander

1 tbsp (15 ml) vegetable oil

1 tsp balsamic vinegar

1½ lbs (680 g) chicken wings

BBQ GLAZE

1 tbsp (15 ml) olive oil

1 clove garlic, diced

½ tsp paprika

½ tsp ground coriander

½ tsp smoked paprika

⅓ cup (80 ml) ketchup

2 tbsp (30 ml) apple cider vinegar

1 tbsp (15 ml) Worcestershire sauce

2 tbsp (30 ml) molasses or honey

⅓ cup (80 ml) water

You can never go wrong with chicken wings; they are such a crowd-pleaser. These wings are smothered in rich, sticky homemade barbecue sauce and are slightly crispy on the outside and tender and juicy on the inside. Sure, you could use store-bought barbecue sauce, but it is so much better to make your own at home. You can adjust the seasoning easily, and it takes less than 5 minutes to make it. Serve these sticky chicken wings as an appetizer for gatherings, parties, and birthday celebrations along with a cold drink. Or serve them as a main dish for a simple weeknight dinner accompanied with fries and a big bowl of seasonal salad for some freshness.

Arrange racks in the middle and at the top of the oven, then preheat it to 450°F (230°C).

For the chicken wings, in a bowl, combine the paprika, coriander, oil, and vinegar. Rub the mixture all over the chicken wings. Arrange the chicken wings on a sheet pan, then roast the wings on the middle rack of the oven for 20 minutes.

Prepare the BBQ glaze while the chicken roasts. Put the oil in a saucepan, then place the pan over medium-low heat. Add the garlic, paprika, coriander, and smoked paprika. Stir and cook for a minute, then reduce the heat to low and add the ketchup, vinegar, Worcestershire, molasses, and water. Cook for 5 minutes, stirring occasionally.

Remove the chicken wings from the oven, using gloves to protect from the heat. Change the oven temperature to high broil. Pour half of the BBQ sauce over the chicken wings. Toss, using a pair of tongs, until the wings are completely coated in sauce. Place them on the top rack of the oven. Broil the wings for 5 minutes, or until they are crispy and caramelized. Serve the chicken wings with the remaining BBQ sauce.

DUCK BREAST
with Plum Chutney

SERVES 4

PREP TIME: 15 minutes

ROASTING TIME:
8–10 minutes

PLUM CHUTNEY
1 lb (450 g) plums, chopped

2 prunes

3 tbsp (45 g) sugar

1 tbsp (15 ml) light soy sauce

2 tbsp (30 ml) rice vinegar

1 clove garlic, minced

1-inch (2-cm) piece ginger, grated

1 star anise

⅔ cup (160 ml) water

1 tbsp (20 g) chili bean paste, such as
La Doubanjiang, optional

ROASTED DUCK
4 (10½-oz [300-g]) boneless duck
breasts, skin on

Salt and freshly ground black pepper

FOR SERVING
Cooked rice

Steamed vegetables

Sliced green onion

Chopped fresh serrano red chile

In Slovenia, we would typically only eat duck for Saint Martin's holiday, which is in November. We wanted to enjoy duck more often, so we created duck recipes that are easy to prepare without taking too much time from the busy schedules we all have. This duck breast recipe has two components: first, the homemade plum chutney that is cooked on the stove, and second, the roasted duck breast, started on the stove and finished in the oven. Flavor-wise, the duck is incredibly tasty, juicy, and gamy with a side of fruity, Asian-inspired, sweet plum chutney.

Arrange a rack in the middle of the oven, then preheat it to 400°F (200°C).

For the plum chutney, put the plums, prunes, sugar, soy sauce, vinegar, garlic, ginger, star anise, water, and chili bean paste, if using, in a saucepan. Bring the mixture to a boil over high heat. Then lower the heat, and simmer the chutney for 20 minutes.

For the roasted duck, pat the duck breasts dry with paper towels. Season the breasts lightly with salt and pepper. Using a sharp knife, score the skin. Make 6 to 8 parallel shallow cuts into the skin. Don't go through the skin. Then, make 6 to 8 shallow cuts in another direction, creating a diamond pattern. Put the duck breasts in a skillet, skin side down. Cook the duck breasts over medium-low heat for 8 to 10 minutes, then turn the duck breasts and cook for another minute.

Transfer the seared duck breasts to a baking sheet, skin side up. Roast the duck breasts on the middle rack of the oven for 8 to 10 minutes, or until a thermometer inserted into the thickest part of the meat registers 135°F (58°C) for medium-rare; 145°F (63°C) for medium; and 160°F (71°C) for well-done. Remove the duck from the oven, and set it aside to rest for 5 minutes.

To serve, brush the duck breasts with the plum chutney. Slice the duck breasts in thin diagonal slices using a sharp knife. Place the duck breasts on top of the rice, with sides of the plum chutney and the vegetables. Garnish with the green onion and serrano red chile.

TANDOORI CHICKEN LEGS
with Spiced Rice

SERVES 4

PREP TIME: 10 minutes

ROASTING TIME: 20 minutes

CHICKEN LEGS

4 small chicken legs, bone in, skin on

¼ cup (60 ml) plain yogurt

⅓ cup (80 ml) heavy cream

1 tbsp (16 g) creamy peanut butter

1 clove garlic, diced

1 tsp garam masala

1 tsp ground ginger

½ tsp paprika

½ tsp ground turmeric

1 tsp freshly squeezed lemon juice

Salt and freshly ground black pepper

SPICED RICE

1 cup (200 g) basmati rice

2½ cups (600 ml) water

⅔ cup (100 g) golden raisins

½ tsp ground turmeric

¼ tsp ground cinnamon

¼ tsp ground allspice

Pinch of salt

FOR SERVING

Plain yogurt

Chopped fresh cilantro, optional

Pomegranate seeds, optional

As are all the dishes in Indian cuisine, this one is incredibly aromatic and full of flavor, with a beautifully crispy skin. Traditionally, Tandoori chicken is made in a tandoor, an outdoor oven with incredibly high heat. We roasted it on the top rack in the oven to achieve a similar, rustic, delicious exterior, while still getting juicy and soft meat. This chicken is paired with a simple spiced rice with raisins.

Arrange a rack at the top of the oven, then preheat it to 450°F (230°C). Line a baking sheet with parchment paper, and set a wire rack on the paper.

For the chicken legs, use a sharp knife to score the chicken skin until you hit a bone. Make four parallel cuts into the skin. Add the chicken legs to a bowl, along with the yogurt, cream, peanut butter, garlic, garam masala, ginger, paprika, turmeric, and lemon juice. Season the marinade with salt and pepper, and rub the mixture into the chicken legs. Set aside the chicken legs for 5 minutes (see Note).

Remove the chicken legs from the marinade, and place them on the rack on the prepared pan. Set aside the marinade.

Place the chicken on the top rack of the oven. Roast the legs for 10 minutes. Remove the pan from the oven, and brush the chicken generously with the marinade. Flip over the chicken legs, return them to the oven, and roast for 5 minutes.

Prepare the spiced rice while the chicken is roasting. Put the rice, water, raisins, turmeric, cinnamon, allspice, and salt in a large saucepan. Place the pan over high heat, cover it with a lid, and bring the mixture to a boil. Then, reduce the heat to low, and let the rice simmer for 11 minutes, or until it's fluffy and all the water is absorbed.

When the chicken legs have finished roasting, remove the pan from the oven. Change the oven temperature to low broil. Brush the chicken legs again with the marinade, and flip them over. Broil the legs on the top rack of the oven for 5 minutes, or until a thermometer inserted into the thickest part of the meat registers 160°F (71°C).

To serve, place a chicken leg and spoonful of rice on each of the four plates. Top the chicken with a dollop of the yogurt, and sprinkle the plate with the cilantro and pomegranate seeds, if using.

NOTE: Feel free to prepare the chicken marinade up to 24 hours before you prepare the chicken. Store the marinade in an airtight container in the refrigerator.

CREAMY CHICKEN LEGS
with Mustard and Leeks

SERVES 4

PREP TIME: 10 minutes

ROASTING TIME:
23–25 minutes

CHICKEN LEGS

4 chicken legs

Salt and freshly ground black pepper

1 tbsp (15 ml) olive oil

2 large leeks, cut into large chunks

2 tbsp (30 ml) Dijon mustard

2 sprigs fresh thyme

1 bay leaf

½ cup (120 ml) Moscato, Vin Santo, or white Port

½ cup (120 ml) heavy cream

FOR SERVING

Chopped fresh chives

Freshly squeezed lemon juice

Mashed potatoes

This is probably our all-time favorite chicken sauce. It is the perfect balance of sweet, sour, and bitter, while still remaining light, fresh, and super creamy. Use the best possible Dijon mustard and a good sweet wine, such as Moscato, Vin Santo, or white Port, to prevent the sauce from being sour. Don't worry, the alcohol will evaporate, and all that will remain will be the inviting aroma and flavor. The chicken is first seared in a pot, then cooked to perfection in the oven. This is a quick and incredibly delicious midweek or weekend dinner.

Arrange a rack in the middle of the oven, then preheat it to 450°F (230°C).

For the chicken legs, separate the drumsticks from the thighs. Season the chicken pieces on both sides with salt and pepper. Put the oil in a large Dutch oven, and heat it over high heat. Place the chicken legs, skin side down, in the pot. Cook the legs for 5 minutes, or until the skin is golden, moving the chicken around from time to time, using tongs.

Add the leeks, Dijon, thyme, bay leaf, and wine to the pot with the chicken. Stir to combine the mixture, and cook it for 2 to 3 minutes, to allow the alcohol to evaporate.

Cover the pot with a lid, and transfer it to the middle rack of the oven. Roast for 15 minutes, then remove the lid and roast for another 8 to 10 minutes, or until a thermometer inserted into the thickest part of the meat registers 160°F (71°C). Remove the pot from the oven, place it over medium heat on the stove, add the heavy cream, and boil the sauce for 3 to 5 minutes.

To serve, divide the chicken and sauce among four plates, then sprinkle it with the chives and lemon juice. Serve the chicken with the mashed potatoes.

NOTE: If the sauce gets very reduced after roasting, add about ⅓ cup (80 ml) of chicken stock or water to the pot when you add the heavy cream.

ROASTED CHICKEN BREAST SALAD

SERVES 4

PREP TIME: 5 minutes

ROASTING TIME: 22 minutes

ROASTED CHICKEN

2 (8–10½-oz [220–300-g]) boneless chicken breasts, skin on

Salt and freshly ground black pepper

1 tbsp (15 ml) olive oil

SALAD

4 handfuls romaine lettuce, chopped

4 handfuls radicchio, chopped

1 handful cherry tomatoes, chopped

1 avocado, chopped

1 red onion, sliced

DRESSING

1 tbsp (15 ml) mayonnaise

1 tbsp (15 ml) olive oil

½ tsp mustard

Salt and freshly ground black pepper

1 tbsp (15 ml) freshly squeezed lemon juice

1 tbsp (5 g) chopped fresh chives

FOR SERVING

Fresh bread, sliced

A simple salad can easily be a very delicious and filling meal, especially if it is served with a juicy, tender roasted chicken. We choose vegetables—lettuce, tomatoes, and avocado—which keep us full for hours and go amazingly well together. You can play around with the salad, adding your favorite vegetables or removing the ones you don't like. This recipe is incredibly flexible. Serve for a light lunch or dinner, or make the salad ahead and take it with you on a trip, to your job, or to school.

Arrange racks in the middle and at the top of the oven, then preheat it to 450°F (230°C).

For the roasted chicken, pat the chicken breasts dry, and place them on a baking sheet. Season the chicken on both sides with salt and pepper. Brush both sides of the chicken with the olive oil. Roast the chicken on the middle rack of the oven for 20 minutes.

While the chicken is roasting, prepare the salad. In a bowl, combine the lettuce, radicchio, tomatoes, avocado, and onion.

For the dressing, in a bowl, stir to combine the mayonnaise, oil, mustard, salt, pepper, lemon juice, and chives. Pour the dressing over the salad, and toss to coat it.

When the chicken has roasted for 20 minutes, change the oven temperature to high broil. Transfer the chicken to the top rack, and broil it for 2 minutes, or until the skin is crispy. Before removing the chicken from the oven, check its temperature. A thermometer inserted into the thickest part of the meat should register 160°F (71°C).

Remove the chicken from the oven, and set it aside to rest for a few minutes before slicing and serving it with the salad and slices of bread.

STICKY MOLASSES TURKEY WINGS

SERVES 4

PREP TIME: 5 minutes

ROASTING TIME: 25 minutes

TURKEY WINGS

8 turkey wings, bone in and butterflied

Salt and freshly ground black pepper

1 tbsp (15 ml) canola oil

MOLASSES GLAZE

2 tbsp (30 ml) ketchup

1 tbsp (15 ml) dark molasses

3 tbsp (45 ml) water

1 tbsp (10 g) Old Bay seasoning

Sweet, sticky, and smoky. These large molasses-glazed turkey wings will quickly become your game-day favorite. By roasting them in the oven for the first 15 minutes, we ensure that the turkey wings will get cooked, and by glazing them two separate times while roasting, the molasses glaze will remain delicious and inviting, instead of burnt and too browned. These turkey wings are comfort food at its finest, great for weeknight dinners, game days, or picnics. Serve them with a fresh seasonal salad and a cold beverage.

Arrange racks in the middle and at the top of the oven, then preheat it to 450°F (230°C). Place a wire rack over a baking sheet.

Place the turkey wings on a cutting board. Using a sharp knife, cut each turkey wing at the thickest part along the bone until you can open the turkey wing like a book.

Place the wings on the wire rack, skin side up. Season them with salt and pepper, and drizzle them with the oil. Place the pan on the middle rack of the oven. Roast the wings for 15 minutes.

While the turkey wings are roasting, make the molasses glaze. In a small bowl, stir to combine the ketchup, molasses, water, and Old Bay seasoning.

When the wings have roasted for 15 minutes, remove them from the oven. Change the oven temperature to low broil.

Brush the turkey wings with the molasses glaze, then broil the wings on the top rack of the oven for 5 minutes. Remove the wings from the oven, turn the wings over, and brush them again with the glaze. Roast the wings for 5 minutes. Before removing the wings from the oven, check the temperature of the turkey. A thermometer inserted into the thickest part of the meat should register 160°F (71°C).

EPIC PORK MADE IN NO TIME

By choosing the right cut of meat, you can drastically reduce the roasting time of pork, without compromising on the flavor and texture. We managed to use a lot of different cuts of meat in this book. The trick is to choose the high-quality, smaller parts of the meat, which are also less pricey. Remember, the better the ingredients, the better the flavor of the dish, so try buying organic ingredients when possible.

We have some of our family classics in this book, such as Smoky Beans with Roasted Pork Sausages (page 96), which is a simple and incredibly quick, hearty meal, especially when served with a slice of bread. Then, we have the most delicious Swedish Pork Meatballs with Gravy (page 107). The fluffy, bite-size meatballs can easily be prepared in advance, and they make a wonderful freezer-friendly meal. Pork Polpette and Tomato Sauce Sandwich (page 95) will soon become your all-time favorite. This Roman-inspired sandwich is the best example of how high-quality, simple ingredients—prepared correctly—can make a rich and luxurious meal. Last, but definitely not least, all pork lovers should try the Mustardy Pork Tenderloin Roast in Mushroom Sauce (page 91). The meat is juicy, tender, and soft, while the creamy mushroom sauce takes the dish to another level, with its rich flavor and celebration of the best of what autumn has to offer.

AROMATIC STUFFED PORK LOIN ROAST

SERVES 4

PREP TIME: 5 minutes

ROASTING TIME:
25–30 minutes

PORK

1 cup (30 g) mixed fresh herbs, such as sage, rosemary, thyme, and parsley

½ cup (60 g) dried apricots or cranberries

Salt and freshly ground black pepper

1 tbsp (6 g) panko breadcrumbs

1½–2 lbs (680–900 g) boneless blade-end pork loin roast, butterflied

1 tbsp (15 ml) olive oil

FOR SERVING

Green Bean Salad with Mustard Dressing (page 150) or Crispy Roasted Potatoes (page 171)

Maple Syrup–Glazed Rutabaga with Pancetta (page 157)

Gravy (page 226)

There is nothing more glamorous than an aromatic, stuffed pork loin roast, also known as porchetta. This magnificent piece of roasted meat deserves the center position on your dinner table because it truly is a showstopper. Tender, juicy roasted pork with crispy, golden-brown skin and a sweet, herby stuffing make this the perfect main dish for all kinds of autumn and winter celebrations and holidays. Now you can make it in 30 minutes by choosing the right, smaller cut of meat and by roasting it at a high temperature.

Arrange a rack in the middle of the oven, then preheat it to 480°F (250°C).

For the pork, in a blender or food processor, combine the herbs, apricots, a pinch of salt, a pinch of pepper, and the panko. Pulse until the mixture is crumbly and combined, about 30 seconds. Set aside the mixture.

Place the butterflied pork loin (as seen in photos 1, 2, and 3) on a baking sheet. Season it with salt and pepper on both sides. Spread the stuffing over one side of the pork (as seen in photo 4). Roll the meat lengthwise (as seen in photo 5). Using kitchen string, tie the pork tightly, with the strings 1 inch (2 cm) apart (as seen in photo 6). Drizzle the pork all over with the oil.

Roast the stuffed meat on the middle rack of the oven for 25 to 30 minutes, or until a thermometer inserted into the thickest part of the meat registers 135°F (58°C).

Remove the stuffed pork loin from the oven. Let the meat rest for a few minutes, then slice it, and serve it warm with the green bean salad, rutabaga, and gravy.

NOTES: Feel free to use a center pork loin cut or suckling pig loin cut; however, make sure that the meat isn't thicker than 1 inch (2 cm) when it's butterflied and laid out. If it's thicker, pound it with a rolling pin to the thinner measurement before spreading over the stuffing, to ensure the proper roasting time.

If you prefer your pork well-done, cut it in slices after the meat has rested, then sear it in a nonstick pan with a bit of oil until it's golden brown.

SWEET AND SOUR PEANUT PORK LOIN

SERVES 4

PREP TIME: 10 minutes

ROASTING TIME: 15 minutes

Over here in Slovenia, it is hard to order Chinese food takeout, so we need to get creative, roll up our sleeves, and make it ourselves. Something that we absolutely adore is sweet and sour pork or chicken. It is such a delicious, incredibly flavorful, and colorful dish that is great for a quick and delicious weeknight dinner served with steamed rice and vegetables.

PORK

12½-oz (360-g) boneless pork loin, cut into thin strips

Salt and freshly ground black pepper

½ tsp garlic powder

1 mango, cut into 1-inch (2-cm) chunks

1 onion, sliced

1 red bell pepper, stemmed, seeded, and sliced

1 yellow bell pepper, stemmed, seeded, and sliced

4 tbsp (36 g) peanuts

2 tbsp (30 ml) vegetable or sesame oil

SWEET AND SOUR SAUCE

1 tbsp (8 g) cornstarch

1 cup (240 ml) water or apple juice

3 tbsp (45 ml) ketchup

1 tbsp (15 ml) white wine vinegar or rice vinegar

2 tbsp (30 ml) freshly squeezed lime juice

1 tsp freshly grated ginger

1 clove garlic, diced

2 tbsp (30 g) brown sugar

1 tbsp (15 ml) light soy sauce

Salt and freshly ground black pepper, to taste

FOR SERVING

Steamed rice

2 green onions, chopped, optional

Steamed vegetables, optional

Arrange a rack at the top of the oven, then preheat it to high broil. Line a baking sheet with parchment paper.

For the pork, season the meat with salt, pepper, and the garlic powder. On the prepared baking sheet, toss together the pork, mango, onion, red pepper, yellow pepper, and peanuts. Drizzle the mixture with the oil to lightly coat all of the ingredients.

Place the pan on the top rack of the oven, and broil the pork and vegetables for 10 minutes, or until the meat and vegetables start to brown in spots.

Make the sweet and sour sauce while the pork and vegetables roast. In a saucepan, whisk the cornstarch and water until the cornstarch dissolves. Add the ketchup, vinegar, lime juice, ginger, garlic, brown sugar, and soy sauce. Place the pan over medium-high heat, and bring the sauce to a boil. Reduce the heat to low and cook, whisking continuously, for 5 minutes, or until the sauce is slightly thickened and covers the back of the spoon. Season the sauce with salt and pepper, to taste.

When the pork and vegetables have roasted until they start to brown in spots, remove the pan from the oven. Pour the sauce over the meat and vegetables, then return the pan to the oven, on the top rack, and broil for another 5 minutes, or until the sauce is slightly thickened.

To serve, top the rice with the pork and vegetable mixture and some green onions, if using. Serve with the steamed vegetables, if using.

RED CURRY-GLAZED PORK CUTLETS

with Roasted Cabbage

SERVES 4

PREP TIME: 5 minutes

ROASTING TIME:
18–22 minutes

ROASTED CABBAGE

2 tbsp (28 g) unsalted butter, softened

½ tsp cumin seeds

½ tsp fennel seeds

Salt and freshly ground black pepper

½ head cabbage, cored and cut into quarters

1 tbsp (15 ml) vegetable oil

PORK CUTLETS

4 (1-inch [2-cm]-thick) boneless pork cutlets

Salt and freshly ground black pepper

2 tbsp (30 g) red curry paste

1 tbsp (15 ml) olive oil

FOR SERVING

Honey Mustard Sauce (page 227)

Overcooked cutlets tend to be dry and dull. But by roasting them in the oven for a shorter period of time on a high temperature, we achieve a perfectly cooked pork cutlet that remains juicy and tender on the inside and beautifully browned and impressive on the outside. This combination works tremendously well. We have slightly spicy pork along with sweet, earthy cabbage. Don't forget to spoon over the honey mustard sauce: it's game-changing. This meal is a quick and easy weeknight dinner for any day of the week.

Arrange a rack in the top of the oven, then preheat it to 450°F (230°C). Grease a baking sheet.

For the cabbage, in a small bowl, combine the butter, cumin seeds, fennel seeds, salt, and pepper until the mixture is well blended. Place the cabbage on the prepared baking sheet. Drizzle it with the oil, then rub the butter mixture into the cabbage. Put the pan on the top rack of the oven. Roast the cabbage for 10 to 12 minutes, or until it's slightly charred but still crunchy.

While the cabbage is roasting, prepare the meat. Pat the pork cutlets dry using paper towels. Season them with salt and pepper on both sides. Stir together the curry paste and olive oil, then brush the mixture on both sides of the pork.

When the cabbage is slightly charred, remove it from the oven, and change the oven temperature to high broil.

Push the cabbage to one side of the baking sheet. Place the cutlets on the empty side of the baking sheet. Return the pan to the top rack of the oven, and broil the pork and cabbage for 8 to 10 minutes, or until a thermometer inserted into the thickest part of the meat registers 135°F (58°C) and the cabbage is nicely charred and caramelized. Turn over the pork cutlet once while it is roasting.

Serve the cutlets and cabbage with the Honey Mustard Sauce.

ROASTED PORK TENDERLOIN
with Celery Salad

SERVES 4

PREP TIME: 5 minutes

ROASTING TIME: 20–22 minutes

PORK TENDERLOIN

2 (1-lb [450-g]) pork tenderloins, trimmed

Salt and freshly ground black pepper

1 tsp ground cumin

1 tsp dried marjoram

1 tsp ground coriander

1 tsp paprika

1 tbsp (5 g) cumin seeds

2 tbsp (30 ml) canola oil

1 bay leaf

CELERY SALAD

1 celery root, peeled and grated

1 handful dried cranberries, chopped

1 tbsp (15 ml) olive oil

¼ cup (60 ml) mayonnaise

1 tsp mustard

2–3 tbsp (30–45 ml) water

1 tbsp (15 ml) freshly squeezed lemon juice

1 tbsp (5 g) chopped fresh chives

¼ tsp freshly grated nutmeg

Salt and freshly ground pepper

FOR SERVING

Gravy (page 226)

This dish brings up so many childhood memories. Growing up with Austrian culinary influence—Maja's grandma's way of cooking—I became very familiar with traditional dishes, such as rich, creamy celery root salad and spiced pork roasts. This type of cooking is home to me, and the flavors are on point. Juicy pork tenderloin, wholly coated in spices, and the simple side with both sweet and tart flavors make a beautifully balanced meal for any day of the year, for all seasons and occasions.

Arrange a rack in the middle of the oven, then preheat it to 450°F (230°C).

For the pork tenderloins, sprinkle them with the salt, pepper, ground cumin, marjoram, coriander, paprika, and cumin seeds. Rub the mixture into the meat.

Transfer the pork tenderloins to a deep baking dish. Drizzle them with the oil. Pour ⅓ cup (80 ml) of water into the baking dish. Add the bay leaf to the dish, and place it on the middle rack of the oven. Roast the meat for 20 to 22 minutes, or until a thermometer inserted into the thickest part of the meat registers 135°F (58°C).

While the pork is roasting, make the celery salad. In a large bowl, combine the celery root, cranberries, oil, mayonnaise, mustard, water, lemon juice, and chives. Season with the nutmeg and salt and pepper, to taste. Toss the ingredients to disperse the seasonings.

Remove the roasted pork from the oven, and let it rest for a few minutes. Then slice it, plate it, and top it with the gravy. Serve it with the celery root salad.

MISO-APRICOT-GLAZED PORK CHOPS
with Bean Salad

SERVES 4

PREP TIME: 10 minutes

ROASTING TIME: 8–10 minutes

MISO-APRICOT GLAZE

1 tbsp (15 ml) canola oil

2 cloves garlic, sliced

½ cup (165 g) apricot jam

1 tbsp (20 g) miso paste

1 tbsp (15 ml) light soy sauce

¼ cup (60 ml) water

2 tbsp (30 ml) white wine vinegar

ROASTED PORK CHOPS

4 (12-oz [340-g]) bone-in pork chops

Salt and freshly ground black pepper

1 tbsp (15 ml) olive oil

BEAN SALAD

2 (15-oz [425-g]) cans borlotti or cannellini beans, drained

1 shallot, finely diced

1 handful parsley, chopped

¼ tsp paprika

2 tbsp (30 ml) olive oil

1 tbsp (15 ml) freshly squeezed lemon juice

1 small head radicchio, leaves separated and cut into large pieces

Salt and freshly ground black pepper

The sweet and slightly sour glaze that is coating these pork chops is out-of-this-world delicious. The apricot jam complements the pork chops beautifully, but make sure to choose a high-quality apricot jam that isn't mostly sugar. This meat—juicy and perfectly cooked, with a golden-brown exterior—is paired with a side of a simple bean salad to add some freshness and lightness to the dish. Better yet, this simple, healthy weeknight dinner is packed with flavor and easy to make in less than twenty minutes.

Arrange a rack in the middle of the oven, then preheat it to 410°F (210°C).

For the miso-apricot glaze, put the oil in a small saucepan, and set it over medium-high heat. Add the garlic, stir, and cook it for 30 seconds. Add the jam, miso, soy sauce, water, and vinegar and stir again. Bring the mixture to a boil, then reduce the heat and simmer the glaze for 5 minutes.

Season the pork chops with salt and pepper. Place a large, ovenproof cast-iron skillet over high heat. When the skillet is hot, add the oil and pork chops. Sear them on both sides, 2 to 3 minutes per side.

Remove the pork chops from the heat. Spoon 2 tablespoons (30 ml) of the miso-apricot glaze onto each pork chop, then rub the glaze into the meat. Roast the chops on the middle rack of the oven for 8 to 10 minutes, or until a thermometer inserted into the thickest part of the meat registers 135°F (58°C).

While the pork chops are roasting, make the bean salad. In a bowl, combine the beans, shallot, parsley, paprika, oil, lemon juice, and radicchio. Stir to combine the ingredients, then season the salad with salt and pepper, to taste, and stir again.

Remove the pork chops from the oven, and set them aside to rest for 5 minutes. Divide the chops among four plates, and serve them with the salad and the remaining miso-apricot glaze.

MUSTARDY PORK TENDERLOIN ROAST
in Mushroom Sauce

SERVES 4

PREP TIME: 15 minutes

ROASTING TIME:
12–15 minutes

PORK

2 (1-lb [450-g]) pork tenderloins, trimmed

Salt and freshly ground black pepper

4 tbsp (60 ml) olive oil, divided

3 tbsp (42 g) unsalted butter

2 tbsp (30 ml) Dijon mustard

MUSHROOM SAUCE

1 tsp olive oil

1 onion, diced

4 cloves garlic, sliced

1 lb (450 g) fresh or frozen mixed mushrooms, such as porcini and portobello, sliced

1 sprig thyme

1 tsp all-purpose flour

½ cup (120 ml) Moscato, Vin Santo, or white Port

¾ cup (180 ml) heavy cream

½ cup (120 ml) chicken or beef stock

FOR SERVING

Chopped fresh parsley

The flavor of this roast is rich, earthy, and so creamy, thanks to the heavy cream. The tenderloin is glazed with mustard and roasted to perfection. The exterior is golden brown, while the interior is juicy, soft, and tender. It is a beautiful weeknight or weekend dinner for colder days. Serve this dish with mashed potatoes, pasta, or gnocchi.

Arrange a rack in the middle of the oven, then preheat it to 450°F (230°C).

For the pork, place a large skillet over high heat. Place the pork in a large bowl, and season it with salt and pepper. Drizzle the pork with 2 tablespoons (30 ml) of the olive oil, and rub the seasoning into the meat.

When the pan is hot, add the butter and the remaining 2 tablespoons (30 ml) of olive oil. Place the tenderloins in the pan and sear them on all sides, 1 to 2 minutes per side. Transfer the pork to a baking sheet, along with the cooking juices. Reserve the skillet.

Brush the meat with the mustard. Roast the pork on the middle rack of the oven for 12 to 15 minutes, or until a thermometer inserted into the thickest part of the meat registers 135°F (58°C).

While the pork is roasting, prepare the mushroom sauce. Place the skillet back over medium-high heat, and add the oil, onion, and garlic. Cook them for 2 to 3 minutes, stirring occasionally. Then add the mushrooms and thyme. Cook for 5 minutes on high heat, or until the mushrooms are slightly browned. Add the flour and stir. Add the wine, and cook it for about 2 minutes, or until the alcohol evaporates and the wine is reduced by about two-thirds. Pour in the cream and stock. Bring the mixture to a boil, then simmer it until the sauce thickens, about 5 minutes.

Remove the pork from the oven and let it rest for 2 to 3 minutes.

To serve, transfer the mushroom sauce to a serving platter. Slice the pork tenderloin and add it to the platter. Spoon some mushroom sauce over the meat. Sprinkle with the parsley, and serve immediately.

NOTE: If you use frozen mushrooms, make sure to cook them for a couple of minutes longer to ensure they are well cooked.

BLACKENED PORK TENDERLOIN TACOS

SERVES 4

PREP TIME: 5 minutes

ROASTING TIME:
16–18 minutes

PORK

1 lb (450 g) pork tenderloin, trimmed

1 tbsp (15 ml) vegetable oil

1 tsp smoked paprika

1 tsp paprika

¼ tsp freshly ground black pepper

½ tsp salt

½ tsp ground coriander

½ tsp dried oregano

¼ tsp allspice

¼ tsp garlic powder

½ tsp cumin

¼ tsp chili powder, optional

1 tsp Dutch process cocoa powder

FOR SERVING

Warm tortillas

Guacamole

Finely sliced lettuce

Grated carrots

Sliced jalapeños

Chopped fresh tomatoes

Salsa Roja (page 229)

Chopped cucumbers

It is hard to believe that this pork tenderloin was not cooked outside on a hot barbecue grill. It is smoky with a blackened exterior that is full of spices and flavor. Roasting it at a high temperature at first will result in that beautiful, dark exterior, but after we lower the heat for a couple of minutes, we achieve the perfectly cooked, tender, juicy interior. Cut the pork tenderloin into very thin slices and serve it wrapped in a warm tortilla, along with your favorite taco toppings. It is such a simple dinner that it can be made any day of the week, and for parties and gatherings, too.

Arrange a rack in the middle of the oven, then preheat it to 450°F (230°C).

For the pork, place the tenderloin on a baking sheet, and brush it with the oil. In a bowl, stir to combine the smoked paprika, paprika, pepper, salt, coriander, oregano, allspice, garlic powder, cumin, chili powder, if using, and cocoa. Rub the mixture all over the pork tenderloin.

Roast the pork on the middle rack of the oven for 8 to 10 minutes, then reduce the oven temperature to 390°F (200°C). Roast the meat for 8 minutes, or until a thermometer inserted into the thickest part of the meat registers 135°F (58°C). Remove the pork from the oven, let it rest for 5 minutes, then cut it into thin slices.

To serve, put the pork slices into the tortillas, and top the pork with the guacamole, lettuce, carrots, jalapeños, tomatoes, salsa, and cucumbers.

PORK POLPETTE AND TOMATO SAUCE SANDWICH

SERVES 6

PREP TIME: 15 minutes

ROASTING TIME:
14–16 minutes

PORK POLPETTE

1 slice white bread, crusts removed and bread cut into cubes

1 tbsp (5 g) chopped dried porcini mushrooms

⅓ cup (80 ml) lukewarm milk

1 lb (450 g) ground pork

1 onion, diced

1 tbsp (5 g) chopped fresh parsley

1 anchovy fillet

1 egg

Salt and freshly ground black pepper

TOMATO SAUCE

1 tbsp (15 ml) olive oil

½ onion, diced

1 carrot, peeled and grated

1 celery rib, grated

1 clove garlic, grated

14 oz (400 g) canned chopped tomatoes

¼ cup (60 ml) water

½ tsp dried oregano

Salt and freshly ground black pepper

This pork is tender with a subtle dried porcini flavor that will immediately transport you to Italy. The tomato sauce is incredibly simple yet packed with vegetables and flavors. Serve for a picnic, a dinner party, or a simple midweek dinner along with a bowl of seasonal salad.

FOR SERVING

2 French baguettes, cut into 3 pieces each, then cut lengthwise to form a sandwich pocket

Olive oil, optional

Shaved Parmesan cheese, optional

Chopped fresh parsley, optional

Arrange racks in the middle and at the top of the oven, then preheat the oven to 450°F (230°C). Grease a baking sheet.

For the polpette, in a small bowl, combine the bread, mushrooms, and milk. Set the mixture aside to soak. In a large bowl, combine the pork, onion, parsley, anchovy, and egg. Knead the mixture with your hands until everything is well combined. Season the mixture with salt and pepper. Add the soaked bread mixture, and knead it into the meat until the mixture is smooth. Divide the mixture into twelve pieces. Using wet hands, roll the mixture into round meatballs, then press them together to get a polpette, or patty. Place the polpette on the prepared baking sheet.

Roast the polpette on the middle rack of the oven for 12 to 14 minutes, or until the meat is cooked through and lightly browned.

While the meat is roasting, make the tomato sauce. Put the oil in a skillet, and set it over medium-high heat. Add the onion, carrot, celery, and garlic. Stir and cook the ingredients for 2 to 3 minutes. Then add the tomatoes, water, and oregano. Season the sauce with salt and pepper. Stir, and cook for 5 minutes.

When the meat is cooked through and lightly browned, change the oven temperature to high broil, move the pan to the top rack, and broil the polpette for 2 minutes, or until the meat is nicely caramelized and brown.

To serve, remove the roasted polpette from the oven. Spread some tomato sauce over both cut sides of the bread pocket. Place two polpette on top of the tomato sauce. Drizzle the sandwiches with the olive oil, if using, and sprinkle them with the Parmesan and parsley, if using.

SMOKY BEANS
with Roasted Pork Sausages

SERVES 4

PREP TIME: 5 minutes

ROASTING TIME:
25 minutes

ROASTED PORK SAUSAGES

4 pork sausages (about 1 lb [450 g])

2 tbsp (30 ml) olive oil

Salt and freshly ground black pepper

1 tsp cumin seeds

1 tsp fennel seeds

SMOKY BEANS

1 tbsp (15 ml) vegetable oil

1 onion, diced

1 carrot, diced

¼ celery rib, diced

1 clove garlic, diced

1 tsp paprika

1 tsp smoked paprika

1 tbsp (15 ml) ketchup

2 (15-oz [425-g]) cans borlotti or
cannellini beans, drained

½ (200 g) can tomato passata or
tomato puree

1 tsp brown sugar

2 leaves fresh sage

½ cup (120 ml) water

Salt and freshly ground black pepper

FOR SERVING

Chopped fresh parsley, optional

Crème fraîche or sour cream, optional

Sourdough bread

We used to eat roasted beans with tomato sauce at least once a month when we were kids. It was a simple, quick, and easy-to-make dish, served with a slice of dark bread. In this recipe, we take it to the next level by adding a favorite pork sausage, and we make it smoky by adding some smoked paprika.

Arrange a rack at the top of the oven, then preheat it to 430°F (220°C). Grease a baking sheet.

For the sausages, place the sausages on the prepared baking sheet, and drizzle them with the oil. Season with salt and pepper, and sprinkle the sausages with the cumin and fennel seeds. Roast the sausages on the top rack of the oven for 10 minutes.

Prepare the smoky beans while the sausages roast. Place an ovenproof skillet over medium-low heat. Add the oil, onion, carrot, and celery. Stir, and cook for 3 minutes, then add the garlic, paprika, and smoked paprika. Stir, and cook for 1 minute. Stir in the ketchup, beans, tomato passata, brown sugar, sage, and water. Season with salt and pepper.

Transfer the roasted pork sausages, with the roasting juices, from the baking sheet to the skillet with the beans. Roast the sausages and beans on the top rack of the oven for 15 minutes, or until the sausages are crispy.

To serve, sprinkle the dish with the parsley, if using, and add a spoonful of the crème fraîche, if using. Serve the beans and sausages with the bread.

SAGE PORK CHOPS
with Apple-Carrot Salad

SERVES 4

PREP TIME: 10 minutes

ROASTING TIME:
6–8 minutes

PORK CHOPS

4 (10½-oz [300-g]) pork chops

Salt and freshly ground black pepper

1 tbsp (5 g) fennel seeds

2 tbsp (30 ml) olive oil, divided

6–8 fresh sage leaves

2 cloves garlic, crushed

APPLE-CARROT SALAD

2 carrots, thinly sliced

1 apple, cored and thinly sliced

1 bunch watercress

½ cup (50 g) chopped walnuts or pecans

2 tbsp (30 ml) olive oil

1 tbsp (15 ml) freshly squeezed lemon juice

1 tsp Roasted Sesame Seed Paste (page 236)

Salt and freshly ground black pepper

APPLE CIDER SAUCE

1 tbsp (15 ml) Dijon mustard

1 tbsp (15 ml) honey

½ cup (120 ml) apple cider

Pork chops are a great cut of meat to prepare when you lack time: They need little prep and cook really fast. In late autumn, we usually get the best organic pork from a nearby farm, so we like to use autumn ingredients to bring out all the flavors and juiciness of the high-quality meat. Sweet flavors go tremendously well with pork, so don't skip the apple cider sauce. And definitely take advantage of the short roasting time to make the simplest apple-carrot salad. It's slightly sweet and a healthy side for juicy, flavorful sage-scented pork chops.

Arrange a rack in the middle of the oven, then preheat it to 450°F (230°C).

For the pork chops, season the meat with salt, pepper, and the fennel seeds. Drizzle the pork with 1 tablespoon (15 ml) of the oil. Rub the seasoning into the meat. Place a large ovenproof skillet over high heat. When the skillet is scorching, add the remaining 1 tablespoon (15 ml) of oil and the pork chops. Cook for 2 minutes, then turn the pork chops and add the sage and garlic. Cook for 2 minutes.

Roast the pork chops on the middle rack of the oven for 6 to 8 minutes, or until a thermometer inserted into the thickest part of the meat registers 135°F (58°C).

While the pork chops are roasting, prepare the salad. In a bowl, stir to combine the carrots, apple, watercress, and walnuts. Drizzle the olive oil, lemon juice, and Roasted Sesame Seed Paste over the salad. Season it with salt and pepper, and toss together the ingredients.

Remove the pork chops from the oven, transfer them to a plate, and let them rest for 5 minutes. Place the skillet, with the roasting juices, over medium-low heat. Be careful; the skillet is very hot. Use protective kitchen gloves. Add the mustard, honey, and cider to the skillet with the roasting juices. Stir, bringing the mixture to a boil, and cook it for 2 to 3 minutes, or until the sauce is reduced by half.

Divide the pork chops among four plates, pour the sauce over the meat, and serve it with the apple-carrot salad.

COCONUT PORK NECK SKEWERS

SERVES 4

PREP TIME: 5 minutes

ROASTING TIME:
12–13 minutes

PORK NECK

1½ lbs (680 g) pork neck, cut into
¼-inch (6-mm)-thick slices

2 cloves garlic, minced

1 tsp freshly grated ginger

1 tsp brown sugar

1 tbsp (15 ml) canola oil, plus more for
drizzling

1 tsp freshly grated lime zest

1 tbsp (15 ml) freshly squeezed lime
juice

1 tbsp (15 ml) oyster sauce

1 tbsp (15 ml) light soy sauce

Salt and freshly ground black pepper

¼ cup (60 ml) coconut milk

FOR SERVING

Fresh cilantro

Cucumber salad

Not a summer goes by without us grilling pork neck outside. This cut of meat is tasty and, because of the amount of fat, it never becomes dry or dull. Pork neck skewers are so delicious that it would be sad to limit them to summertime. That's why we decided to make summer-inspired pork neck skewers that can be cooked in an oven, even when the weather won't allow us to grill outside. They are cooked right under the broiler, which helps them develop a tasty, charred flavor that is just lip-smacking delicious. By brushing the skewers with coconut milk while broiling, you take them to the next level with little time and effort.

Arrange a rack at the top of the oven, then preheat it to high broil. Grease a baking sheet. If you are using wooden skewers, cover them with water in a shallow pan to soak them for 10 minutes.

For the pork neck, in a large bowl, combine the meat, garlic, ginger, brown sugar, oil, lime zest, lime juice, oyster sauce, and soy sauce. Lightly season the mixture with salt and pepper. Rub the mixture into the meat.

Thread the pork neck slices onto parallel metal or wooden skewers, with the skewers 1 inch (2 cm) apart. Place the skewers on the prepared baking sheet. Drizzle canola oil over the skewers.

Broil the pork on the top rack of the oven for 6 minutes. Brush the skewers with the coconut milk, turn over the skewers, then broil for 3 minutes. Brush the meat with coconut milk again, then broil for 3 to 4 minutes, or until the meat is nicely caramelized. Remove the skewers from the oven.

To serve, transfer the skewers to a serving platter, sprinkle them with the cilantro, and serve with the cucumber salad.

ROASTED PORK BELLY TACOS

SERVES 4

PREP TIME: 5 minutes

ROASTING TIME:
18–20 minutes

ROASTED PORK BELLY

1½-lb (680-g) skinless, boneless pork belly, cut into ½-inch (1-cm) cubes

1 tbsp (15 ml) olive oil

1 tsp coriander seeds

½ tsp ground cumin

1 tsp paprika

Salt and freshly ground black pepper

MANGO SALSA

1 mango, diced

2 tbsp (2 g) chopped fresh cilantro

1 red onion, thinly sliced

1 jalapeño, diced

1 tbsp (15 ml) freshly squeezed lime juice

Salt and freshly ground black pepper

FOR SERVING

Warm tortillas

Chopped tomatoes, optional

Salsa Roja (page 229)

Oh my goodness, there is so much flavor in roasted pork belly! These crispy, super-juicy pork belly bites are served in a warm tortilla with homemade mango salsa and chopped tomatoes. I mean, what's not to love? This is a simple, quick, flavorful, and vibrant meal that will make all of your family members extremely excited and happy for dinner. It's all made in under 25 minutes, so you can easily prepare it during a busy week, for gatherings, parties, or Taco Tuesday.

Arrange a rack in the middle of the oven, then preheat it to 450°F (230°C).

Arrange the pork belly on a baking sheet, drizzle it with the oil, then sprinkle on the coriander seeds, cumin, paprika, salt, and pepper. Rub the seasonings into the meat.

Roast the pork belly on the middle rack of the oven for 18 to 20 minutes, or until it's golden brown and crisp. Stir the meat halfway through the cooking time.

While the pork is roasting, make the mango salsa. In a bowl, stir to combine the mango, cilantro, onion, jalapeño, and lime juice. Season with salt and pepper, and set aside the salsa.

To serve, fill the tortillas with the meat, and top it with the mango salsa, tomatoes, if using, and Salsa Roja.

GLAZED PORK BELLY
with Broccoli Basmati Rice

SERVES 4

PREP TIME: 5 minutes

ROASTING TIME:
25 minutes

ROASTED PORK BELLY

2 tbsp (30 ml) hoisin sauce

1 tbsp (15 ml) rice vinegar

1 tbsp (15 ml) soy sauce

1 tbsp (15 g) light brown sugar

1 clove garlic, minced

1 tsp freshly grated ginger

1 lb (450 g) skinless, boneless pork belly, cut into two long strips

BROCCOLI BASMATI RICE

1 cup (220 g) basmati rice

2⅔ cups (640 ml) water

1 tsp freshly grated ginger

1 star anise

4 spring onions, chopped

1 handful Chinese broccoli or broccoli florets

FOR SERVING

Peanut Butter Sauce (page 233), optional

Sriracha

Sesame seeds

Chinese-inspired glazed pork belly is magnificent. We coat moist, tender pork meat in a sweet and slightly sour glaze that gives it a little extra kick. The pork absorbs all those flavors during roasting. We love pairing this pork belly with light and fluffy basmati rice with spring onion and broccoli to add some freshness to the dish. It's a quick and easy weeknight dinner menu for all Chinese food lovers.

Arrange racks in the middle and at the top of the oven, then preheat it to 430°F (220°C). Line a baking sheet with parchment paper.

For the pork belly, in a bowl, stir to combine the hoisin sauce, vinegar, soy sauce, brown sugar, garlic, and ginger. Brush the pork with half of the glaze, then transfer the meat to the prepared baking sheet. Set aside the remaining glaze.

Roast the pork belly on the middle rack of the oven for 15 minutes; stir the meat halfway through the cooking time. Remove the pork from the oven, and brush it with the remaining glaze.

While the pork is roasting, make the basmati rice. Bring the rice, water, ginger, and star anise to a boil in a saucepan over medium heat. Then, cover the pan with a lid, lower the heat, and simmer for 8 minutes. Remove the lid, and add the spring onions and broccoli. Cook for another 3 minutes, or until the vegetables are slightly cooked and the rice is fluffy.

When the pork belly has roasted for 15 minutes, change the oven temperature to high broil, then broil the pork on the top rack of the oven for 10 minutes, or until a thermometer inserted into the thickest part of the meat registers 155°F (68°C).

To serve, remove the pork belly from the oven and slice it. Divide the rice among four plates, then arrange the pork belly slices on top of the rice. Serve the dish with the Peanut Butter Sauce, if using, and a drizzle of sriracha, for some extra spiciness. Garnish with sesame seeds.

SWEDISH PORK MEATBALLS
with Gravy

SERVES 4

PREP TIME: 15 minutes

ROASTING TIME: 12 minutes

ROASTED MEATBALLS

1 tbsp (15 ml) canola oil

1 onion, diced

1 clove garlic, diced

2 tbsp (12 g) panko breadcrumbs

⅔ cup (160 ml) heavy cream

½ tsp ground cloves

½ tsp ground allspice

½ tsp freshly grated nutmeg

Salt and freshly ground black pepper

1 lb (450 g) ground pork

GRAVY

2 tbsp (28 g) unsalted butter

2 tbsp (18 g) all-purpose flour

2 cups (480 ml) beef stock

⅓ cup (80 ml) heavy cream

Salt and freshly ground black pepper

FOR SERVING

Mashed potatoes

Parsley, chopped

Cooked vegetables

These are just the best pork meatballs we have ever made or eaten. They are such a crowd-pleaser, and you simply won't be able to resist making these at least once a month. The soft, roasted, bite-sized pork is served with hearty, incredibly tasty homemade gravy. It is the ultimate comfort food, made in just 30 minutes. We serve these with mashed potatoes and some cooked vegetables. However, in Sweden, they serve them with lingonberry sauce—cranberry sauce will work, too— and sometimes gherkins. Make them for a comforting family weeknight dinner.

Arrange racks in the middle and at the top of the oven, then preheat it to 450°F (230°C). Grease a baking sheet.

For the meatballs, in a small skillet, heat the oil over medium-low heat. Add the onion, stir, and cook for 2 to 3 minutes, then add the garlic and cook for another 2 to 3 minutes, stirring occasionally.

In a large bowl, combine the panko with the heavy cream. Add the onion mixture— reserving the skillet—cloves, allspice, and nutmeg. Season with salt and pepper. Add the ground pork to the bowl, and stir well, until the mixture is smooth. Divide the mixture into 32 pieces. Using wet hands, roll the mixture into round meatballs, and place them on the prepared baking sheet.

Roast the meatballs for 10 minutes on the middle rack of the oven. Change the oven temperature to high broil, then transfer the meatballs to the top rack, and broil them for 2 minutes, or until they are slightly browned.

While the meatballs are roasting, make the gravy. In the skillet you used for the onion mixture, melt the butter over medium-low heat. Add the flour, stir, and cook for 5 minutes on low heat, or until the mixture is slightly brown. While whisking, gradually pour in the beef stock, and bring the mixture to a boil. Cook for 2 to 3 minutes, or until the gravy is slightly thickened. Add the heavy cream, and season with salt and pepper.

To serve, plate the mashed potatoes on four plates, top them with the meatballs, and pour the gravy over all of it. Sprinkle with parsley and serve with the cooked vegetables.

NOTE: You can make these meatballs ahead. Freeze the shaped, uncooked meatballs in a freezer bag for up to 2 months. The roasting time is 5 minutes longer for frozen meatballs.

MOUTH-WATERING FISH AND SEAFOOD MADE EASY

Fish and seafood roasts are not only the easiest to make, but they are also the lightest and healthiest recipes in this book. Fresh fish is absolutely best, but if you use frozen fish, make sure to defrost it completely before cooking it. To help you always get the juiciest, tastiest fish, we wrote a general rule on how to roast round and white fish. That simple rule will help you achieve delicious results always, no matter the size of the fish.

You will find exciting recipes, such as Stuffed Squid with Bread, Capers, and Tomato Sauce (page 113), in this chapter. The squid is stuffed with bread and other delicious ingredients, then roasted in a short period of time to achieve a delightful texture. Cornmeal-Crusted Trout with Braised Cabbage (page 125) is an updated childhood classic that is roasted in the oven instead of fried with a large amount of oil in the pan, making it lighter and healthier. And if you want something that's showstopping and impossible to resist, definitely try the Roasted Cajun Shrimp with Butter Sauce (page 121). It's addictive, and it makes a beautiful, quick appetizer or snack when you have friends or family over.

When possible, choose fish that are local and fresh; they are the most flavorful.

HONEY MUSTARD-GLAZED SALMON FILLET

SERVES 4

PREP TIME: 5 minutes

ROASTING TIME:
16–20 minutes

Such a fancy-looking dinner, made in minutes. Not only is this salmon fillet glazed with a beautiful honey mustard mixture, but it is also served with a light topping made from fresh herbs and lemon. The citrusy aroma complements this sweet fish beautifully. The juicy and flaky salmon fillet will impress all of your dinner guests, and it will not take a lot of time or skill for you to make it. This is a great recipe for both beginners and those who are more advanced in the kitchen.

SALMON

1 (2-lb [900-g]) whole fresh salmon fillet

Salt and freshly ground black pepper

1 tbsp (15 ml) olive oil

1 tsp Dijon mustard

1 tsp yellow American mustard

1 tbsp (15 ml) honey

1 tbsp (15 ml) freshly squeezed lemon juice

HERB TOPPING

1 tbsp (5 g) chopped fresh chives

1 tbsp (5 g) chopped fresh dill

2 tbsp (30 ml) olive oil

1 tbsp (5 g) freshly grated lemon zest

1 tbsp (15 ml) freshly squeezed lemon juice

FOR SERVING

Chopped fresh red chile, such as serrano, optional

Tabbouleh salad or cooked couscous

Arrange racks in the middle and at the top of the oven, then preheat it to 320°F (160°C). Line a baking sheet with parchment paper.

For the salmon, place the fillet on the prepared baking sheet. Season it with salt and pepper, then drizzle it with the oil.

Slow-roast the salmon on the middle rack of the oven for 14 to 16 minutes, or until a thermometer inserted into the thickest part of the fish registers 118°F (48°C).

While the fish is roasting, make the honey mustard glaze. In a bowl, stir to combine the Dijon mustard, American mustard, honey, and lemon juice.

For the topping, in a bowl, combine the chives, dill, oil, and lemon zest and juice.

Remove the fish from the oven. Change the oven temperature to high broil. Brush the salmon generously with the honey mustard glaze. Roast the salmon on the top rack of the oven, under the broiler, for 2 to 4 minutes, or until golden on top.

To serve, spoon the herb topping over the roasted salmon fillet, then sprinkle it with the chile, if using. Serve the dish with the tabbouleh salad.

STUFFED SQUID
with Bread, Capers, and Tomato Sauce

SERVES 4

PREP TIME: 10 minutes

ROASTING TIME:
20 minutes

STUFFED SQUID

4 thick slices stale white sandwich
bread, cut into cubes

½ cup (120 ml) milk

4 (4-oz [115-g]) squid, cleaned, bodies
and tentacles separated (see Note)

½ onion

4 cloves garlic

1 tbsp (15 g) capers

1 bunch parsley, chopped

2 tbsp (30 ml) olive oil

1 egg

1 tbsp (6 g) breadcrumbs

Salt and freshly ground black pepper

TOMATO SAUCE

1 tbsp (15 ml) olive oil

½ onion, chopped

2 cloves garlic, sliced

3 tbsp (45 g) capers

1 cup (240 g) tomato passata or
tomato puree

1 cup (240 ml) water or fish stock

Salt and freshly ground black pepper

1 bay leaf

Roasting squid in the oven is quick and simple, and it gets that beautifully charred flavor that's specific to barbecue. We top this dish with a delightful, light homemade tomato sauce with capers; it complements the squid beautifully. As a side, cook tagliatelle pasta or make creamy polenta.

Arrange a rack in the middle of the oven, then preheat it to 430°F (220°C). Line a baking sheet with parchment paper.

For the squid, put the bread in a medium bowl, pour the milk on it, then set aside the bowl.

In the bowl of a food processor, combine the squid tentacles, onion, garlic, capers, and chopped parsley. Pulse until the onion is finely chopped and the mixture is combined. Transfer the mixture to the bowl with the soaked bread. Add the olive oil, egg, and breadcrumbs. Stir well to combine. Season with salt and pepper and stir again.

Pat the squid bodies dry using paper towels. Stuff about three-quarters of each squid with the prepared mixture. Thread the top with a toothpick to close the squid tightly. Creating a small hole (as seen in photo 5) helps the steam to release while roasting and prevents the filling from bursting out of the squid while in the oven.

Transfer the stuffed squid to the prepared baking sheet, then roast it on the middle rack of the oven for 10 minutes. Turn over the squid, and roast them for 10 minutes, or until they are golden brown and tender.

While the squid roasts, make the tomato sauce. In a saucepan, heat the oil over medium-low heat. Add the onion, stir, and cook it for 5 minutes. Add the garlic and capers, stir, and cook for 1 minute. Stir in the tomato passata and water. Season the sauce with salt, pepper, and the bay leaf. Cook the sauce for 10 minutes, or until the sauce is rich and slightly thickened.

Remove the stuffed squid from the oven, and serve it with the tomato sauce.

NOTE: If you are using cleaned squid without the tentacles, chop an extra squid to add to the food processor for the stuffing.

Also, feel free to use twelve small squid—2 ounces (55 g) each—instead of four larger ones. Roast the smaller squid for 5 to 8 minutes on each side, or until the squid is golden brown and tender.

SIMPLY ROASTED PORGY

SERVES 4

PREP TIME: 5 minutes

ROASTING TIME:
18–20 minutes

PORGY

2 fresh porgies, cleaned

½ tsp sea salt

2 slices lemon

1 tbsp (15 ml) olive oil

Salt and freshly ground black pepper

SAUCE

½ cup (120 ml) Chardonnay or other
dry or semidry wine

1 clove garlic, minced

¼ cup (60 ml) olive oil

1 handful parsley, roughly chopped

Salt and freshly ground black pepper

FOR SERVING

Crispy Roasted Potatoes (page 171)

Green Bean Salad with Mustard
Dressing (page 150)

It's called porgy in America, we call it sea bream, and the French call it *daurade*. No matter what you call it, this is a delicious fish that we beautifully complement with a light sauce—made from fresh garlic, white wine, parsley, and olive oil.

Arrange a rack in the middle of the oven, then preheat it to 450°F (230°C). Line a baking sheet with parchment paper.

For the porgy, pat the fish dry using paper towels, then put the fish on the prepared baking sheet. Season the cavity of the fish with the sea salt, and tuck in the lemon. Drizzle the fish with the olive oil on both sides. Lightly sprinkle the fish with salt and pepper.

Roast the fish on the middle rack of the oven for 18 to 20 minutes, or until a thermometer inserted into the thickest part of the fish registers 125°F (52°C). See below for Pro Tips for Roasting Fish.

While the fish is roasting, make the sauce. In a saucepan, bring the wine and garlic to a boil over medium-high heat. Cook the mixture for 2 to 3 minutes so that the alcohol evaporates. Remove the white wine mixture from the heat, and stir in the olive oil. Transfer the mixture to a small bowl, add the parsley, and season the sauce with salt and pepper.

Serve the roasted fish with the sauce, potatoes, and green bean salad.

PRO TIPS FOR ROASTING FISH

We've created a foolproof, simple-to-follow roasting method that works well for many varieties of fish, including yellowfin bream, sea or striped bass, salmon, snapper, trout, haddock, pollock, red or common mullet, mackerel, and cod.

Our simple rule for timing is to start with a baseline of roasting the fish for 6 minutes. Add another 6 to 8 minutes of roasting for every 10½ ounces (300 g) of fish. Roast the fish on the middle rack at 450°F (230°C).

It's best to use a thermometer before taking the fish from the oven. Checking the internal temperature helps prevent overcooking, which ensures the juiciness of the fish. The fish is ready when a thermometer inserted into the thickest part of the fish registers 125°F (52°C).

If your fish is thicker than 1½ inches (4 cm), cut two to three diagonal slices about ½ inch (1 cm) deep into the skin. This helps the fish cook evenly.

SLOW-ROASTED LEMON TROUT FILLET

with Caper Salsa

SERVES 4

PREP TIME: 10 minutes

ROASTING TIME:
12–15 minutes

TROUT

4 (8½–12½-oz [240–350-g]) fresh trout fillets

Salt and freshly ground black pepper

1 tbsp (15 ml) canola oil

8 thin lemon slices

CAPER SALSA

2 tbsp (30 ml) olive oil

4 shallots or 1 red onion, thinly sliced

4 cloves garlic, thinly sliced

¼ cup (60 g) capers

3 tbsp (42 g) unsalted butter

1 tbsp (15 ml) freshly squeezed lemon juice

1 tsp freshly grated lemon zest

Salt and freshly ground black pepper

FOR SERVING

Chopped fresh parsley

Béarnaise Sauce (page 230), optional

Oh, this lemon trout fillet is just divine. This tender, soft, citrusy trout fillet is roasted to perfection and topped with a simple capers-based salsa that is tangy, fresh, and delicious. This lemon trout roast is perfectly light for summer, yet comforting enough for colder days. Serve it for dinner parties or weeknight dinners, as soon as it comes out of the oven. As a side, we recommend cooked potatoes.

Arrange a rack in the middle of the oven, then preheat it to 320°F (160°C). Line a baking sheet with parchment paper.

For the trout, place the fillets on the prepared baking sheet. Season the fish with salt and pepper, and drizzle it with the oil. Place two slices of lemon on each fillet.

Roast the fish on the middle rack of the oven for 12 to 15 minutes, or until a thermometer inserted in the thickest part of the fish registers 130°F (54°C) and the fish is flaky and separates easily with a fork.

While the fish is roasting, make the caper salsa. Place a saucepan over medium-high heat, then add the oil, shallots, and garlic and cook for 2 to 3 minutes. Add the capers, stir, and cook for 2 minutes. Then add the butter and let it melt. Remove the sauce from the heat, drizzle in the lemon juice, and sprinkle in the lemon zest. Season with salt and pepper, to taste.

To serve, transfer the roasted trout to a serving platter. Spoon the caper salsa on top of it, then sprinkle it with the parsley. Serve with the Béarnaise Sauce, if using.

MOROCCAN ROASTED SALMON

SERVES 4

PREP TIME: 10 minutes

ROASTING TIME:
14–18 minutes

SALMON

1 tbsp (15 ml) canola oil

1 onion, diced

4 cloves garlic, diced

½ tsp ground ginger

½ tsp ground cumin

½ tsp paprika

½ tsp ground turmeric

¼ tsp ground cinnamon

1 roasted red bell pepper from a jar, sliced

½ tsp chopped preserved lemon

1 bay leaf

7¼ oz (205 g) canned diced tomatoes

½ cup (120 ml) water

1 large tomato, chopped

Chopped leaves of 1 bunch fresh parsley

Salt and freshly ground black pepper

4 (6–8-oz [170–220-g]) fresh salmon fillets

1 tbsp (15 ml) olive oil

FOR SERVING

Cooked couscous

Chopped fresh herbs

4 lemon wedges

This simple and healthy dish is packed with spiced vegetables and flaky, perfectly cooked salmon. The roasted red bell pepper and preserved lemon give subtle yet aromatic, exotic flavors to the sauce. The salmon is simply seasoned with salt and pepper, to celebrate its naturally sweet and specific taste. The cooked couscous will soak up all of the tasty sauce.

Arrange a rack at the top of the oven, then preheat it to 480°F (250°C).

For the salmon, place a skillet over medium-low heat. Add the canola oil and onion. Cook for 3 minutes, stirring occasionally. Add the garlic, ginger, cumin, paprika, turmeric, and cinnamon, and cook for 1 minute. Add the bell pepper, preserved lemon, bay leaf, diced tomatoes, water, tomato, and parsley. Season with salt and pepper, and bring the mixture to a boil.

Pat the salmon fillets dry using paper towels. Season them with salt and pepper, then drizzle them with the olive oil. Transfer the vegetable mixture to an ovenproof baking dish. Place the salmon fillets on top, skin side up. Roast the salmon on the top rack of the oven for 14 to 18 minutes, or until a thermometer inserted into the thickest part of the fish registers 118°F (48°C).

Spoon the couscous onto each of four plates, then top it with a salmon fillet and one-quarter of the vegetable mixture. Sprinkle the herbs over the plates, then add a lemon wedge to each one.

ROASTED CAJUN SHRIMP
with Butter Sauce

SERVES 4

PREP TIME: 15 minutes

ROASTING TIME:
8–10 minutes

CAJUN SEASONING

2 tbsp (10 g) paprika

½ tsp smoked paprika

1 tsp garlic powder

1 tsp dried oregano

1 tsp dried thyme

¼ tsp freshly ground black pepper

1 tsp salt

¼ tsp cayenne

½ tsp dried celery leaves

SHRIMP

¾ cup (170 g) unsalted butter

1 clove garlic, diced

1½ lbs (680 g) whole shrimp, cleaned, deveined, and heads and shells reserved

1 tbsp (15 ml) canola oil

FOR SERVING

Chopped fresh parsley

Grilled bread

4 lemon wedges

Slightly spicy, aromatic, and incredibly flavorful, roasted Cajun shrimp is a luxurious appetizer or lunch. This recipe uses whole shrimp, so we get the most flavor possible. First, we prepare a simple sauce, made from butter, garlic, Cajun seasoning, and shrimp heads. Do not worry: You won't be eating them, but they add flavor to the sauce. The shrimp is coated in homemade Cajun seasoning, then served with the shrimp butter sauce and a wedge of lemon. The three components provide the most delicious explosion of flavors in your mouth.

Arrange a rack at the top of the oven, then preheat it to 450°F (230°C).

For the Cajun seasoning, in a small bowl, stir together the paprika, smoked paprika, garlic powder, oregano, thyme, pepper, salt, cayenne, and celery leaves. Set aside the seasoning.

For the shrimp, set a fine-mesh strainer over a small bowl. Melt the butter in a saucepan over medium-high heat. Add the garlic, 1 tablespoon (10 g) of the Cajun seasoning, and the shrimp heads and shells to the saucepan. Stir well, and cook the mixture over low heat for 5 minutes. Drain the mixture in the prepared strainer, and reserve the butter sauce. Discard the shrimp heads and shells.

Pat the shrimp dry using paper towels. Place them in a bowl. Drizzle them with the oil, then sprinkle them with 2 tablespoons (20 g) of the Cajun seasoning. Rub the mixture into the shrimp.

Transfer the shrimp to a baking sheet. Roast the shrimp on the top rack of the oven for 8 to 10 minutes, or until it's pink and opaque.

To serve, sprinkle the shrimp with the parsley, and serve it with a side of the shrimp butter sauce, bread, and a lemon wedge.

NOTE: You can prepare this recipe even faster by substituting 1 tablespoon (10 g) of Old Bay seasoning for the Cajun seasoning in the butter sauce and 2 tablespoons (20 g) to coat the shrimp.

LEMON SARDINES
with Herb Sauce

SERVES 4

PREP TIME: 5 minutes

ROASTING TIME:
14–16 minutes

Not only are these roasted sardines healthy, crispy, and delicious, but they are easy to make on a hectic weeknight, and they keep you full for hours. This recipe is made in less than twenty minutes, and it can be served as an appetizer or for a light lunch or dinner. Sardines are affordable and incredibly rich nutritionally, as they are full of healthy fats. Not only that, but they also taste amazing. Serve them with the homemade herb sauce in the recipe, grilled bread, and a seasonal salad.

SARDINES

2 lbs (900 g) whole fresh sardines, scaled and cleaned

4 slices fresh lemon

1 tbsp (15 g) capers

2 tbsp (30 ml) olive oil

½ tsp paprika

Salt and freshly ground black pepper

HERB SAUCE

3 tbsp (15 g) chopped fresh parsley or cilantro

3 tbsp (45 ml) olive oil

2 tbsp (30 ml) freshly squeezed lemon juice

Pinch of salt

Pinch of freshly ground black pepper

¼ fresh red chile, such as serrano, chopped

4 green olives, pitted and chopped

1 ripe tomato, squeezed

Arrange racks in the middle and at the top of the oven, then preheat it to 450°F (230°C).

For the sardines, put the sardines, lemon slices, and capers on a baking sheet. Drizzle them with the oil and paprika, then season them with salt and pepper. Roast them on the middle rack of the oven for 12 to 14 minutes, or until they are cooked through and juicy inside.

While the sardines are roasting, make the herb sauce. In a bowl, stir to combine the parsley, oil, lemon juice, salt, pepper, chile, olives, and tomato. Set aside.

When the sardines are cooked through, change the oven temperature to high broil. Broil the sardines on the top rack for 2 minutes, or until they are crisp and slightly grilled outside.

Remove the sardines from the oven, transfer them to a serving platter, and drizzle them with the herb sauce.

CORNMEAL-CRUSTED TROUT

with Braised Cabbage

SERVES 4

PREP TIME: 10 minutes

ROASTING TIME: 17–20 minutes

TROUT

2 (1-lb [450-g]) whole fresh trout or arctic char

1 tbsp (15 ml) canola oil

Salt and freshly ground black pepper

½ cup (61 g) cornmeal

BRAISED CABBAGE

1 tbsp (15 ml) olive oil

½ small head cabbage, cored and roughly chopped

2 carrots, thinly sliced

1 clove garlic, diced

1 tbsp (15 ml) light soy sauce

1 tsp apple cider vinegar

Salt and freshly ground black pepper

FOR SERVING

4 lemon wedges

Chopped fresh red chile, such as serrano, optional

Chopped fresh cilantro, optional

Giving trout a crispy cornmeal coating is one of the best ways to prepare this delicious, juicy fish. Usually, we would pan-fry the trout with oil. Roasting it in the oven requires less oil, so the preparation is healthier, and we still achieve that lip-smacking, tender interior and crispy, crusted exterior. Since the prep and roasting don't take a lot of time, it is a great dinner choice for super-busy days when you want something delicious and healthy for yourself and your family. We pair the trout with a quick and straightforward, flavorful braised cabbage and carrots.

Arrange racks in the middle and at the top of the oven, then preheat it to 450°F (230°C). Line a baking sheet with parchment paper.

For the trout, place the fish on a tray or a large plate. Drizzle it with the oil, and season it with salt and pepper on both sides. Spread the cornmeal on a plate, then roll the fish in the cornmeal until it is completely coated on both sides. Transfer the fish to the prepared baking sheet.

Roast the fish on the middle rack of the oven for 15 to 18 minutes, or until the fish is tender and flaky. Change the oven temperature to high broil, and broil the fish on the top rack for 2 minutes, or until the fish is crispy and flaky, and the flesh is easily separated with a fork (see Note).

While the trout is roasting, make the braised cabbage. Heat the oil in a skillet over medium-high heat. Add the cabbage and cook it for 3 to 5 minutes, stirring occasionally. Add the carrots, garlic, soy sauce, and vinegar, then season the mixture with salt and pepper. Stir the mixture, cover the pan with a lid, and cook the braise for 5 minutes, or until the vegetables are crisp-tender when tested with a knife.

Remove the trout from the oven. Divide the fish among four plates, and add one lemon wedge and a serving of the cabbage to each plate. Sprinkle the braised cabbage with the chile and cilantro, if using.

NOTE: The cooking time in the recipe is based on two 1-pound (450-g) trout. If your fish is much smaller or larger, follow a simple rule to roast this fish. Start by roasting the fish for 6 minutes, then add another 6 to 8 minutes of roasting for every 10½ ounces (300 g) of fish.

ROASTED MUSSELS
with Fennel and Wine

SERVES 4

PREP TIME: 10 minutes

ROASTING TIME:
8–10 minutes

Mussel dishes hold a very special place in our hearts. Traditionally in our area, the Adriatic Sea, mussels are served with a fresh tomato sauce or a simple white wine sauce, such as the one in this recipe. The goal when cooking mussels is to get a creamy, flavorful sauce and juicy and delicious mussels. They are cooked incredibly fast, so they make a great midweek dinner, but they are still fancy enough for you to serve them to guests.

MUSSELS

2 tbsp (30 ml) olive oil

4 cloves garlic, diced

1 large fennel bulb, cored and very thinly sliced

1 bunch fresh parsley, finely chopped

2 sun-dried tomatoes, finely chopped

1 tbsp (15 g) capers

2 tbsp (12 g) breadcrumbs

¾ cup (180 ml) Chardonnay or other dry or semidry wine

3½ lbs (1½ kg) fresh mussels, cleaned and sorted (see Note)

Arrange a rack in the middle of the oven, then preheat it to 450°F (230°C).

For the mussels, place a heavy roasting pan over medium-low heat. Add the oil and garlic, and cook for a minute. Add the fennel, parsley, tomatoes, and capers, then stir and cook for 2 to 3 minutes. Add the breadcrumbs, cook for 1 minute, then add the wine. When the wine comes to a boil, add the mussels. Arrange the mussels in two layers, cover the pan with a lid or foil, then remove it from the heat.

Roast the mussels on the middle rack of the oven for 8 to 10 minutes, or until all of the shells are opened.

To serve, transfer the mussels and fennel to a large serving dish. Sprinkle the parsley over the dish, and serve the mussels with the baguette.

FOR SERVING

Chopped fresh parsley

French baguette

NOTE: To clean mussels, place them in a colander and run them under cold running water. Some people also soak them in two to three bowls of cold water, draining them between soakings, and scrub them with a brush to remove any sand. Sort the mussels to remove any mussels with broken shells, or that are already open, a sign that the mussel is dead.

ROASTED MACKEREL ESCABÈCHE

SERVES 4

PREP TIME: 8 minutes

ROASTING TIME: 15–18 minutes

MACKEREL

4 (1-lb [450-g]) fresh mackerel fillets, (see Note)

Salt and freshly ground black pepper

2 tbsp (30 ml) olive oil

SAUCE

1 tbsp (15 ml) olive oil

2 shallots or 1 onion, sliced

2 cloves garlic, diced

½ fresh red chile, such as serrano, sliced

1 red bell pepper, stemmed, seeded, and cut into strips

1 yellow bell pepper, stemmed, seeded, and cut into strips

2 carrots, cut into strips

¾ cup (180 ml) freshly squeezed orange juice

¼ cup (60 ml) sherry vinegar

⅓ cup (80 ml) Chardonnay or other dry or semidry wine

2 cloves

Salt and freshly ground black pepper

FOR SERVING

Olive oil

Chopped fresh cilantro or parsley, optional

This is the most colorful fish recipe in this cookbook. The beautiful, vibrant colors from the escabèche sauce are incredibly inviting, and the fish is juicy and tender with a rich flavor. This sauce is both sweet and slightly sour, creating a beautiful balance between the citrusy orange flavor and the sherry vinegar. It's a light and fresh dish that can be served warm or cold and needs a slice of fresh bread.

Arrange a rack in the middle of the oven, then preheat it to 450°F (230°C). Line a baking sheet with parchment paper.

For the mackerel, place the fish on the prepared baking sheet, then season it with salt and pepper. Brush the fish with the oil. Roast the fish on the middle rack of the oven for 15 to 18 minutes, or until the fish is flaky and the flesh is easily separated with a fork.

While the fish is roasting, make the sauce. Put the olive oil in a pot, and place it over low heat. Add the shallots, garlic, chile, red and yellow peppers, and carrots. Cook the mixture for 5 minutes, stirring occasionally. Add the orange juice, vinegar, wine, and cloves. Season the sauce with salt and pepper. Bring the sauce to a boil, then set it aside. Before serving, remove the cloves.

To serve, transfer the fish to a serving platter. Spoon the sauce over the fish. Drizzle it with some olive oil, then sprinkle the platter with the cilantro, if using.

NOTE: The cooking time in the recipe is based on four 1-pound (450-g) mackerel. If your fish is much smaller or larger, follow a simple rule to roast this fish. Start by roasting the fish for 6 minutes, then add another 6 to 8 minutes of roasting for every 10½ ounces (300 g) of fish.

Mouthwatering Fish and Seafood Made Easy

ROASTED WHOLE SEA BASS

with Fennel

SERVES 4

PREP TIME: 5 minutes

ROASTING TIME:
15–18 minutes

Sea bass, called branzino in the Mediterranean, is probably the most popular sea fish in Slovenia. It's super easy to prepare, and it takes little time and effort to roast the whole fish. In this recipe, we roast the fish with fennel, cherry tomatoes, olives, and some sourdough bread for extra crunchiness and flavor. All of these Mediterranean flavors work beautifully together and bring out so much flavor from the juicy and tender sea bass.

SEA BASS

2 large fennel bulbs, cored and thinly sliced

2 slices sourdough bread, cut into cubes

6 cherry tomatoes, cut in half

2 tbsp (30 ml) plus 1 tsp olive oil, divided

8 green olives

2 fresh whole sea bass (see Notes)

Salt

FOR SERVING

Crispy Roasted Potatoes (page 171)

Gremolata Sauce (page 234)

Lemon wedges, optional

Arrange a rack in the middle of the oven, then preheat it to 450°F (230°C).

For the sea bass, place the fennel, bread, and tomatoes on a large baking sheet. Drizzle 2 tablespoons (30 ml) of the oil over the ingredients, then add the olives. Toss everything to combine ingredients and coat them with the oil.

Season the sea bass with salt, then drizzle it with the remaining 1 teaspoon of oil. Place the sea bass on top of the vegetables. Roast the fish on the middle rack of the oven for 15 to 18 minutes, or until the fish is flaky and the flesh is easily separated with a fork.

To serve, plate the sea bass with the potatoes, vegetables, and bread, then top the fish and potatoes with the Gremolata Sauce. Serve with lemon wedges on the side, if using.

NOTES: If the fish is thicker than 1½ inches (4 cm), cut two to three diagonal slices about ½-inch (1-cm) deep into the skin to help it cook evenly.

The weight of a whole sea bass can vary. Follow a simple rule to determine how long to roast this fish. Start by roasting the fish for 6 minutes, then add another 6 to 8 minutes of roasting for every 10½ ounces (300 g) of fish.

COD FILLETS
with Tomatoes, Artichokes, and Olives

SERVES 4

PREP TIME: 5 minutes

ROASTING TIME:
22–24 minutes

FOR THE COD

1 lb (450 g) cherry tomatoes

1 (10-oz [285-g]) jar plain cooked artichokes, drained

1 yellow bell pepper, stemmed, seeded, and sliced

1 shallot, quartered

1 handful black olives

1 handful capers

2 tbsp (30 ml) olive oil, divided

Salt and freshly ground pepper

4 (½-lb [220-g]) cod, halibut, or hake fillets

FOR SERVING

Chopped fresh parsley

Freshly squeezed lemon juice

Ground sumac

Béarnaise Sauce (page 230) or Gremolata Sauce (page 234), optional

This healthy Mediterranean dinner will feed your whole family and is a beautiful combination of perfectly cooked, flaky, and tender cod. The fish is served over a medley of colorful vegetables. Feel free to use frozen cod for this recipe, but be sure to defrost it according to the package directions before using it. The dish pairs well with cooked potatoes or fresh bread.

Arrange a rack in the middle of the oven, then preheat it to 450°F (230°C).

For the cod, in a baking dish, combine the tomatoes, artichokes, bell pepper, shallot, olives, and capers. Drizzle the vegetables with 1 tablespoon (15 ml) of the oil, and season with salt and pepper. Toss to combine the ingredients. Roast on the middle rack of the oven for 12 minutes.

Remove the baking dish from the oven, and reduce the temperature to 410°F (210°C). Season the cod with salt, and drizzle it with the remaining 1 tablespoon (15 ml) of oil. Place the fillets over the vegetables in the baking dish. Roast on the middle rack of the oven for 10 to 12 minutes, or until a thermometer inserted into the thickest part of the fish registers 125°F (52°C).

To serve, plate the fish and roasted vegetables, then sprinkle them with the parsley, lemon juice, and sumac. Top the fish with the sauce, if using.

RED MULLET POT ROAST
with Green Beans

SERVES 4

PREP TIME: 5 minutes

ROASTING TIME:
23–25 minutes

MULLET

2 tbsp (30 ml) olive oil

1 onion, diced

2 carrots, cut into ½-inch (1-cm) chunks

1 red bell pepper, stemmed, seeded, and cut into strips

1 tbsp (15 g) capers

2 cloves garlic, diced

1 tsp ground coriander

1 tsp paprika

1 tsp fennel seeds

1 tsp ground turmeric

1 bay leaf

1 tsp freshly squeezed lemon juice

8¾ oz (250 g) canned crushed tomatoes

1½ cups (360 ml) vegetable stock

Salt and freshly ground black pepper

5 oz (150 g) green beans, trimmed

6–8 (4-oz [120-g]) fresh red mullets, cleaned (see Note)

FOR SERVING

1 tbsp (5 g) chopped fresh parsley

Creamy polenta or bread

We would eat this any day of the year. It is an incredibly tasty dish that is not only quick and straightforward; it's pretty healthy. First, we roast the stew in an ovenproof pot, covered, in the center of the oven. Then, we add the delicious, sweet red mullets. The result is fantastic: amazingly roasted, juicy fish, served with a light stew, packed with delicious vegetables.

Arrange racks in the middle and at the top of the oven, then preheat it to 450°F (230°C).

For the mullet, place a Dutch oven over medium-high heat. Add the oil, onion, carrots, bell pepper, and capers. Stir, and cook for 2 to 3 minutes. Add the garlic, coriander, paprika, fennel seeds, turmeric, bay leaf, and lemon juice. Stir the ingredients together, then cook for 1 minute. Add the tomatoes and stock. Season the stew with salt and pepper. Bring the stew to a boil, then add the green beans. Cover the pot, and roast it on the middle rack of the oven for 15 minutes.

Season the mullets with salt and pepper. Remove the lid, add the mullets, and roast the pot on the top rack of the oven for 8 to 10 minutes, depending on the size of the fish. The fish is done when the meat is flaky and the flesh is easily separated with a fork.

To serve, sprinkle the pot with the parsley, and serve the stew over the polenta.

NOTE: If red mullet is not available in your area, feel free to substitute small hake fillets or sea scallops.

UNFORGETTABLE ROASTED VEGGIES

This is definitely the most colorful and vibrant chapter in this book. Roasting vegetables is easy, but in order to make them exciting and fun, we need to get creative with different spices, glazes, and pastes, all of which help the vegetables to develop rich and unique flavors that keep us begging for more.

If you want to incorporate more plant-based meals during the week, you will find delicious recipes in this chapter. We are obsessed with Mushroom Kebabs with Miso Glaze (page 154), an easy and incredibly quick dish that is bursting with umami and is simply unforgettable. Warm your body and soul with Roasted Cauliflower Steaks with Romesco Sauce (page 138). In autumn or winter, serve Creamy Roasted Cabbage with Chorizo (page 141) with your favorite cooked pasta. It's rich, creamy, and incredibly satisfying.

Even if you are the biggest meat lover, we are sure you will find recipes in this chapter that you will love.

ROASTED CAULIFLOWER STEAKS

with Romesco Sauce

SERVES 4

PREP TIME: 5 minutes

ROASTING TIME:
20 minutes

Switch your beef steak with this simple roasted cauliflower steak for a quick, easy, and delicious midweek dinner. When we roast cauliflower, it becomes sweet, slightly charred, and crunchy. Romesco sauce, which is fresh, light, and colorful, tops the cauliflower to give us a beautiful combination of completely different textures and flavors that work wonderfully together. For some extra crunchiness, we top the steaks with pine nuts and, for some freshness, sprinkle them with fresh parsley.

CAULIFLOWER

1 head cauliflower, cut into 1-inch
(2-cm)-thick steaks

3 tbsp (45 ml) olive oil

¼ tsp ground cumin

¼ tsp garlic powder

¼ tsp dried oregano

½ tsp smoked paprika

Salt and freshly ground black pepper

1 tbsp (10 g) pine nuts

FOR SERVING

Freshly squeezed lemon juice

Romesco Sauce (page 232)

Fresh parsley

Arrange a rack in the middle of the oven, then preheat it to 430°F (220°C).

Place the cauliflower steaks on a baking sheet. Drizzle them with the oil, and season them with the cumin, garlic powder, oregano, paprika, salt, and pepper. Rub the seasoning into the cauliflower steaks.

Roast the steaks on the middle rack of the oven for 10 minutes. Turn the cauliflower steaks, using a fish spatula or a fork, and sprinkle them with the pine nuts. Roast for 10 minutes, or until the steaks are tender when tested with a fork.

To serve, plate the roasted cauliflower steaks, drizzle them with the lemon juice, spoon the Romesco Sauce over them, then sprinkle them with the parsley.

CREAMY ROASTED CABBAGE
with Chorizo

SERVES 4

PREP TIME: 10 minutes

ROASTING TIME:
20–23 minutes

We are always on the lookout for new pasta sauces, especially in the autumn and winter, when there aren't many seasonal vegetables around or in the garden. Cabbage not only stores well in a cold place, but it also stays in season for a long time, offering us the opportunity to experiment while still eating seasonally. In this recipe, the cabbage is roasted, served with a creamy, incredibly delicious sauce, and sprinkled with chorizo. It makes a beautiful side for celebrations or a midweek dinner, and it also makes a rich sauce served over cooked tagliatelle pasta.

CABBAGE

1 tbsp (15 ml) olive oil

1 head cabbage, cored and cut into
2-inch (4-cm)-thick wedges

½ cup (80 g) Spanish smoked chorizo,
cut into ½-inch (1-cm) cubes

1 clove garlic, crushed

1 tbsp (14 g) unsalted butter

1 onion, diced

1 clove garlic, minced

1 tsp all-purpose flour

1 cup (240 ml) milk

1 cup (240 ml) chicken stock or water

Salt and freshly ground black pepper

¼ tsp freshly grated nutmeg

1 bay leaf

¼ cup (25 g) grated Parmesan cheese

FOR SERVING

Cooked pasta

Chopped fresh parsley, optional

Freshly squeezed lemon juice, optional

Arrange a rack in the middle of the oven, then preheat it to 430°F (220°C).

For the cabbage, heat the olive oil in a large pan over medium-high heat. Add the cabbage, chorizo, and crushed garlic. Cook the cabbage for 2 to 3 minutes, then turn the cabbage wedges, and cook for 2 minutes.

Transfer the cabbage wedges to a baking dish. Pour the cooking juices over the cabbage, leaving the chorizo and garlic in the pan. Roast the cabbage on the middle rack of the oven for 15 to 18 minutes, or until the cabbage is slightly charred and almost cooked.

Cook the chorizo and garlic on the stove for 2 to 3 minutes, until they are golden brown and crispy. Transfer the cooked chorizo to a plate, using a slotted spoon.

Add the butter, onion, and minced garlic to the pan. Cook for 2 minutes, then add the flour, stir it in, and cook on low heat for 5 minutes. Increase the heat to medium-low, and pour in the milk and chicken stock. Using a whisk, stir the mixture continuously while bringing it to a boil; the whisking prevents any lumps from forming. Season the sauce with salt and pepper, then stir in the nutmeg and bay leaf. Cook the sauce over medium-high heat for 5 minutes to thicken it.

Remove the roasted cabbage from the oven, then pour the creamy sauce over it. Sprinkle the cabbage with the chorizo and the Parmesan. Return the cabbage to the oven, and roast it for 5 minutes, or until golden brown.

Spoon the mixture over the cooked pasta, then sprinkle the dish with the parsley and lemon juice, if using.

MISO-GLAZED EGGPLANT

SERVES 4

PREP TIME: 5 minutes

ROASTING TIME: 22 minutes

EGGPLANT
2 eggplants
1 tbsp (15 ml) canola oil

MISO MARINADE
2 tbsp (30 ml) canola oil
4 cloves garlic, minced
1-inch (2-cm) piece ginger, grated
1 tbsp (20 g) miso paste
¾ cup (180 ml) water
1 tbsp (15 ml) light soy sauce
3 tbsp (45 ml) rice vinegar or white wine vinegar
1 tbsp (15 g) brown sugar

FOR SERVING
Chopped peanuts
Sesame seeds
Green onions
Crushed red pepper, optional

This is probably the most aromatic eggplant dish we have ever eaten. The flavor is just incredibly luxurious and so inviting. I could eat this dish every week, spooned over rice or soba noodles, or just simply served as a side to any pork or chicken roast. The preparation is quick and easy, and the seasonings create the unbelievable umami flavor that we all want to taste every day.

Arrange a rack in the middle of the oven, then preheat it to 450°F (230°C).

Slice the eggplants crosswise into 3-inch (8-cm) pieces, then quarter the pieces lengthwise. Arrange the pieces on a baking sheet, then drizzle them with the oil. Roast the eggplant on the middle rack of the oven for 12 minutes, turning once while roasting.

While the eggplant is roasting, make the miso marinade. Heat the oil in a saucepan over medium-low heat. Add the garlic, ginger, and miso paste. Stir, and cook for 30 seconds. Add the water, soy sauce, vinegar, and brown sugar. Bring the mixture to a boil, then reduce the heat, and simmer the marinade for 5 minutes.

Remove the eggplant from the oven, then pour the marinade over it. Roast the eggplant for 10 minutes, or until it's soft when tested with a knife.

To serve, sprinkle the eggplant with the peanuts, sesame seeds, and green onions. Sprinkle the eggplant with the crushed red pepper, if using, for extra spice.

INDIAN-SPICED ROASTED VEGETABLES

SERVES 4

PREP TIME: 5 minutes

ROASTING TIME:
20–25 minutes

ROGAN JOSH PASTE

2 cloves garlic

1 tsp minced ginger

1 tbsp (10 g) garam masala

1 tsp turmeric

1 fresh red chile, such as serrano

1 bunch fresh cilantro

1 tsp ground coriander

1 tsp cumin

1 tbsp (15 g) tomato puree

1 roasted red bell pepper from a jar

1 tbsp (15 ml) canola oil

Salt and freshly ground black pepper

ROASTED VEGETABLES

1 lb (450 g) Hokkaido squash, cut into
½-inch (1-cm)-thick slices

1 lb (450 g) sweet potatoes, cut into
1-inch (2-cm) wedges

1 carrot, cut into chunks

½ cup (120 ml) boiling water

FOR SERVING

Cooked basmati rice

4 sunny-side-up eggs

Chopped fresh cilantro, optional

Toasted coconut chips, optional

Comforting, hearty, and incredibly aromatic, this simple dish can be served as a healthy veggie-packed breakfast alongside a sunny-side-up egg. You can serve it as a side or as a main dish, spooned over cooked basmati rice and topped with a sunny-side-up egg. You will love the aromas that spread from your kitchen when these incredibly versatile rogan josh paste–spiced vegetables are roasting. Feel free to make your own rogan josh paste, which is basically a delicious curry paste, or buy it at your local store.

Preheat the oven to 480°F (250°C).

For the rogan josh paste, in a blender, combine the garlic, ginger, garam masala, turmeric, chile, cilantro, coriander, cumin, tomato puree, red pepper, and oil. Season with salt and pepper. Pulse the blender several times, until you get a smooth paste, then set aside the paste.

For the vegetables, put the squash, sweet potatoes, and carrot in a deep baking dish. Pour the prepared paste over the vegetables, and toss to combine until the vegetables are completely coated. Add the water. Roast the vegetables on the middle rack of the oven for 20 to 25 minutes, or until they are soft when tested with a knife.

To serve, scoop the rice onto four plates, and top each with the vegetables and an egg. Garnish the plates with the cilantro and coconut chips, if using.

NOTE: You can prepare this recipe even faster by substituting 3 tablespoons (45 g) of store-bought rogan josh paste.

ROASTED EGGPLANT
with Hazelnuts and Feta Cheese

SERVES 4

PREP TIME: 10 minutes

ROASTING TIME:
20–25 minutes

ROASTED EGGPLANT

2 medium eggplants

2 tbsp (30 ml) olive oil

1 tsp balsamic vinegar

1 tsp light soy sauce

Salt and freshly ground black pepper

YOGURT SAUCE

4 tbsp (60 ml) Greek yogurt

½ tsp harissa paste

1 tsp freshly squeezed lemon juice

1 tbsp (15 ml) olive oil

1 tbsp (5 g) chopped fresh parsley

Salt and freshly ground black pepper

FOR SERVING

Sesame seeds

Chopped fresh parsley

3 tbsp (30 g) chopped roasted hazelnuts

3 oz (75 g) feta or farmers' cheese

4 pinches of paprika

When it comes to eggplants, we like them stuffed, topped, and full of texture, color, and a lot of flavors. Here in Europe, there are so many delicious eggplant dishes to try: Italian eggplant parmigiana, Greek moussaka, French ratatouille, and many, many others. But we somehow always end up going the Mediterranean route. We roast the eggplant to extract the most flavor possible, and then top it with nuts, seeds, and a generous dollop of light and creamy homemade yogurt sauce. The freshness of yogurt and cheese perfectly balances the rich, intense eggplant. You will love it; we are sure of it.

Arrange a rack in the middle of the oven, then preheat it to 450°F (230°C).

For the eggplant, cut the eggplants in half lengthwise, and score the flesh in a crisscross pattern about ½ inch (1 cm) deep. In a small bowl, combine the oil, vinegar, and soy sauce. Brush the flesh of the eggplants with the mixture, and season the eggplants with salt and pepper. Place the eggplants on a baking sheet, flesh side up.

Roast the eggplant on the middle rack of the oven for 20 to 25 minutes, or until they're soft when tested with a knife. Turn them flesh side down halfway through the cooking time.

For the sauce, in a bowl, combine the yogurt, harissa, lemon juice, oil, and parsley. Season with salt and pepper to taste.

To serve, place the roasted eggplants on a plate, flesh side up, as they come out of the oven. Just before serving, spoon the yogurt sauce on the eggplants, then sprinkle them with the sesame seeds, parsley, and hazelnuts. Top the eggplant with the cheese and paprika.

SQUASH, KALE, AND ISRAELI COUSCOUS SALAD
with Cranberries

SERVES 4

PREP TIME: 5 minutes

ROASTING TIME: 20 minutes

COUSCOUS

1 (1½-lb [680-g]) butternut squash, cut into 1-inch (2-cm) cubes

1 tbsp (15 ml) olive oil

Salt and freshly ground black pepper

½ cup (87 g) Israeli couscous, uncooked

1 bunch raw kale, stemmed and chopped into bite-size pieces

½ cup (50 g) chopped pecans

½ cup (80 g) chopped dried cranberries

SALAD DRESSING

1 tsp Roasted Sesame Seed Paste (page 236)

2 cloves garlic, minced

1 tbsp (15 ml) freshly squeezed lemon juice

¼ cup (60 ml) canola oil

2 tbsp (30 ml) freshly squeezed orange juice

¼ tsp ground cinnamon

¼ tsp ground turmeric

Salt and freshly ground black pepper

This salad is inspired by three of our favorite salads from Whole Foods. It is a mixture of all of them. We have sweet, roasted butternut squash cubes; fresh, raw kale; perfectly cooked Israeli couscous; pecans for crunchiness; and dried cranberries for some extra sweetness and fruitiness. Homemade salad dressing makes all the difference, and it takes only a few minutes to make. It complements the salad well. The dressing is made with homemade tahini (page 236), but feel free to use store-bought tahini if you lack time. This delicious autumn or winter salad is amazing for a quick lunch on the go or a sit-down dinner.

Arrange a rack in the middle of the oven, then preheat it to 450°F (230°C).

For the couscous, spread the butternut squash in a single layer on a baking sheet. Drizzle it with the oil, and sprinkle it with salt and pepper. Toss to combine. Roast the squash on the middle rack of the oven for 20 minutes, or until it's soft when tested with a knife.

While the squash is roasting, cook the couscous according to the instructions on the package.

Make the salad dressing. In a bowl, combine the Roasted Sesame Seed Paste, garlic, lemon juice, oil, and orange juice. Season the dressing with the cinnamon, turmeric, salt, and pepper, and stir to combine.

Remove the roasted squash from the oven, and transfer it to a salad bowl. Add the kale, cooked couscous, pecans, and cranberries. Pour the dressing over the mixture, and stir it until it's well combined.

GREEN BEAN SALAD
with Mustard Dressing

This is one of our favorite green bean salads. It has soft, roasted beans with crunchy sourdough bread cut into cubes and is drizzled with a generous amount of a simple, homemade salad dressing made from Dijon mustard, anchovies, yogurt, Parmesan cheese, and walnuts. Serve this salad for a light lunch, along with Crispy Roasted Chicken Halves (page 48), or as a side for more fancy dinners, such as the Aromatic Stuffed Pork Loin Roast (page 80). Feel free to serve the green bean salad warm or cold.

SERVES 4

PREP TIME: 5 minutes

ROASTING TIME:
15–18 minutes

BEANS

2 lbs (900 g) green beans, trimmed

4 slices sourdough bread, cut into cubes

4 tbsp (60 ml) olive oil

Salt and freshly ground black pepper

MUSTARD DRESSING

1 clove garlic, chopped

2 tbsp (30 ml) Dijon mustard

3 oil-packed anchovy fillets, drained

¼ cup (60 ml) plain yogurt

2 tbsp (30 ml) freshly squeezed lemon juice or vinegar

2 tbsp (13 g) chopped walnuts or pecans

¼ cup (60 ml) vegetable oil

⅓ cup (33 g) freshly grated Parmesan cheese

Salt and freshly ground black pepper

Arrange a rack at the top of the oven, then preheat it to 450°F (230°C).

Toss together the green beans and bread on a baking sheet. Drizzle them with the oil, and season with salt and pepper. Toss to combine.

Roast the beans and bread on the top rack of the oven for 15 to 18 minutes, or until the beans are crisp-tender and the bread is golden brown and crispy. Stir the mixture once or twice while it is roasting.

Make the dressing while the beans roast. In a blender, or using an immersion blender in a bowl, combine the garlic, mustard, anchovies, yogurt, lemon juice, walnuts, oil, and Parmesan. Blend until the mixture is smooth, then season it to taste with salt and pepper.

In a serving bowl, toss together the green bean mixture and the salad dressing.

NOTE: Feel free to add pine nuts, almonds, or walnuts to the green beans when roasting, for some extra crunchiness and nuttiness.

BUFFALO-COATED CAULIFLOWER BITES

SERVES 4

PREP TIME: 5 minutes

ROASTING TIME:
20–25 minutes

ROASTED CAULIFLOWER

1 head cauliflower, broken into small florets

1 tbsp (15 ml) olive oil

½ tsp oregano

¼ tsp garlic powder

Salt and freshly ground black pepper

BUFFALO SAUCE

1 tbsp (15 ml) ketchup

2 tbsp (30 ml) sriracha

¼ tsp garlic powder

1 tsp Worcestershire sauce

½ tsp honey

1 tbsp (15 ml) apple cider vinegar

½ cup (115 g) unsalted butter

Salt and freshly ground black pepper

½ cup (120 ml) heavy cream

FOR SERVING

Chopped fresh parsley

If the Sticky BBQ Chicken Wings (page 67) are the go-to party food for game night and summer gatherings for meat-eaters, then these Buffalo-Coated Cauliflower Bites will become the new go-to party food for all vegetarians. They make a fantastic appetizer, snack, or even a main dish. The cauliflower florets are roasted to perfection, then coated in a rich, extremely creamy homemade buffalo sauce made from simple ingredients. If you have leftover buffalo sauce after coating the cauliflower, use it to dip your roasted bites for extra saucy flavor. Keep it plain and simple and enjoy the bites on their own, or serve them wrapped in a warm tortilla, along with seasonal vegetables.

Arrange a rack in the middle of the oven, then preheat it to 450°F (230°C).

Spread the cauliflower on a small baking sheet. Drizzle it with the oil, and season it with the oregano, garlic powder, salt, and pepper. Toss to combine.

Roast the cauliflower on the middle rack of the oven for 20 to 25 minutes, or until it's crisp-tender.

While the cauliflower is roasting, make the buffalo sauce. In a saucepan, put the ketchup, sriracha, garlic powder, Worcestershire, honey, vinegar, and butter. Place the pan over medium-low heat, and cook the sauce for 1 minute. When the butter is melted, remove the sauce from the heat, and season it with salt and pepper. Add the cream. Using an immersion blender, blend the mixture into a smooth sauce.

Remove the roasted cauliflower bites from the oven, and immediately coat them with the buffalo sauce. Sprinkle the bites with the parsley, and serve them with a side of the remaining buffalo sauce.

MUSHROOM KEBABS
with Miso Glaze

SERVES 4

PREP TIME: 5 minutes

ROASTING TIME:
20 minutes

Mushrooms, one of the most versatile ingredients, can elevate a variety of dishes. In this case, a simple glaze made from miso paste, soy sauce, and maple syrup makes these roasted portobello mushrooms the star of any dinner table. They make a beautiful side, but they can easily be a main dish when served with a simple seasonal salad. The mushrooms are incredibly rich in flavor, aromatic, and have an umami aftertaste.

MUSHROOMS
1 lb (450 g) portobello mushrooms, or any large mushrooms, cut in half

GLAZE
1 tbsp (15 ml) sesame oil
1 clove garlic, diced
1 tbsp (20 g) miso paste
3 tbsp (45 ml) light soy sauce
1 tbsp (15 ml) maple syrup or honey

FOR SERVING
Sesame seeds, optional
Chopped fresh parsley, optional

Arrange a rack in the middle of the oven, then preheat it to 410°F (210°C). If you are using wooden skewers, cover them with water in a shallow pan to soak them for 10 minutes.

Thread the mushrooms onto four metal or wooden skewers. Place the skewers on a baking sheet, and roast them on the middle rack of the oven for 10 minutes.

While the mushrooms are roasting, prepare the glaze. Place a saucepan over medium-low heat. Add the oil, garlic, and miso paste. Stir, and cook for 1 minute. Stir in the soy sauce and maple syrup. Remove the pan from the heat, and set it aside.

Remove the roasted mushrooms from the oven. Pour the roasting juices into the saucepan with the glaze, stir to combine, and brush half of the glaze over the mushroom kebabs. Roast the mushrooms for 10 minutes, or until they are nicely glazed and tender.

Brush the mushrooms with the remaining glaze, and spoon the roasting juices over them. Sprinkle the mushrooms with the sesame seeds and parsley, if using. Serve immediately.

MAPLE SYRUP–GLAZED RUTABAGA
with Pancetta

SERVES 4–6

PREP TIME: 5 minutes

ROASTING TIME:
25 minutes

ROASTED RUTABAGA

2 lbs (900 g) rutabaga, cut into 1-inch (2-cm) chunks

2 tbsp (30 ml) canola oil

2 tbsp (30 ml) maple syrup

Salt and freshly ground black pepper

1 cup (160 g) cubed pancetta (¼-inch [½-cm] cubes)

LEMON DRESSING

1 tsp freshly grated lemon zest

2 tbsp (30 ml) freshly squeezed lemon juice

4 tbsp (60 ml) olive oil

2 tbsp (30 ml) canola oil

Salt and freshly ground black pepper

2 tbsp (10 g) chopped fresh parsley

It is hard to believe that Maple Syrup–Glazed Rutabaga with Pancetta can taste fresh and light, but, honestly, it really does. The citrusy lemon dressing makes all the difference and balances out this dish perfectly. You can easily serve it as a side for autumn and winter holidays. Or, stir it into cooked rice and top it with a sunny-side-up egg for a tasty weeknight dinner. The sweetness from the maple syrup and saltiness from the pancetta complement each other beautifully, while the dressing brings a tangy, citrusy component. It is a crowd-pleaser of a side dish. Everyone will love it.

Arrange a rack in the middle of the oven, then preheat it to 450°F (230°C).

Spread the rutabaga over a baking sheet in a single layer. Drizzle it with the oil and maple syrup. Season with salt and pepper, then roast the rutabaga on the middle rack of the oven for 15 minutes.

While the rutabaga is roasting, make the lemon dressing. In a bowl, stir to combine the lemon zest, lemon juice, olive oil, and canola oil. Season with salt and pepper, and stir in the parsley. Set aside the dressing.

Remove the rutabaga from the oven. Sprinkle the pancetta cubes over the vegetables, and return the pan to the oven. Roast for 10 minutes, or until the pancetta is golden brown and crispy.

Remove the rutabaga with pancetta from the oven. Drizzle the lemon dressing over it, then stir to coat the mixture with the dressing.

CHICORY SALAD
with Golden Raisins

SERVES 4-6
PREP TIME: 5 minutes
ROASTING TIME:
15 minutes

Roasted chicory salad with golden raisins is such an excellent Mediterranean salad for wintertime. Roasted chicory is slightly bitter, so adding a bit of sweetness to it is crucial for a delicate, flavorful balance. We added sweetness by adding large golden raisins to the roasted chicory for the last 3 minutes of roasting and by drizzling honey over the chicory just before serving. This is a beautiful and straightforward salad for during the week but fancy enough to serve for celebrations or when you have friends over.

CHICORY SALAD

4 heads chicory, each halved lengthwise
1 tbsp (15 ml) olive oil
1 tbsp (15 ml) balsamic vinegar
Salt and freshly ground black pepper
¾ cup (109 g) golden raisins

DRESSING

3 tbsp (45 ml) olive oil
1 tbsp (15 ml) freshly squeezed lemon juice
Salt and freshly ground black pepper

FOR SERVING

1 tsp honey
Parmesan cheese, optional

Arrange racks in the middle and at the top of the oven, then preheat it to 430°F (220°C).

For the chicory, arrange the chicory, cut side down, on a baking sheet. Drizzle it with the olive oil and vinegar, and season with salt and pepper.

Roast the chicory for 12 minutes on the middle rack of the oven.

While the chicory is roasting, prepare the dressing. In a bowl, stir to combine the olive oil and lemon juice. Season generously with salt and pepper.

When the chicory has roasted for 12 minutes, remove it from the oven, and change the temperature to 480°F (250°C).

Turn the chicory, and sprinkle it with the raisins. Roast the chicory on the top rack of the oven for 3 minutes, or until it is crisp-tender.

Transfer the roasted chicory to a serving platter, and drizzle the dressing over it, along with the honey. Shave curls of the Parmesan, if using, over the chicory.

ROASTED ORANGE AND FENNEL SALAD

with Feta

SERVES 4

PREP TIME: 5 minutes

ROASTING TIME:
20 minutes

4 oranges, peeled and sliced

4 tbsp (60 ml) olive oil, divided

3 fennel bulbs

1 tbsp (15 ml) sherry vinegar

½ shallot, minced

1 clove garlic, minced

¼ tsp paprika

Salt and freshly ground black pepper

12 black and green olives

2 oz (60 g) feta cheese, optional

You will love this salad. Not only is it incredibly beautiful, colorful, and vibrant, but it tastes even better than it looks. I promise. Roasted oranges are sweet, and the roasted fennel still remains crunchy and slightly bitter, in a good way. The cherry on top, so to speak, is the dressing and crumbled feta. It adds freshness and lightness without overdoing it. It is a simple salad that is perfect for any time oranges are in season, so especially in winter. You can easily make this Mediterranean-inspired salad at home.

Arrange a rack in the middle of the oven, then preheat it to 450°F (230°C).

Arrange the orange slices in a single layer on a baking sheet, and drizzle them with 1 tablespoon (15 ml) of the oil. Roast the oranges on the middle rack of the oven for 20 minutes, or until they are slightly charred and juicy.

Fill a large bowl with ice-cold water. Finely chop the fennel fronds, and set aside 2 tablespoons (5 g) of them. Using a mandoline slicer or a sharp knife, cut the fennel into very thin slices, dropping them in the bowl of water as you slice to keep the fennel crunchy. Set aside the bowl.

While the oranges are roasting, make the salad dressing. In a bowl, stir to combine the remaining 3 tablespoons (45 ml) of oil, the reserved fennel fronds, vinegar, shallot, garlic, and paprika. Season with salt and pepper, and stir until the dressing is smooth.

Drain the fennel, and put it on a serving platter. Remove the oranges from the oven and add them to the platter, along with the olives. Toss to combine the ingredients, then drizzle them with the salad dressing. Crumble the feta cheese over the platter, if using.

FAST SIDES AND APPETIZERS TO SHARE

Jernej is the king of sides, appetizers, and snacks. The more there are on the table, the merrier. We love hosting our friends and family, and we should definitely do it more often. When we do, we like to go all out and make as many different dishes as possible instead of making just one big bowl of a single appetizer or side dish. It's probably because we love food and want to share all the delicious treats with the people we love.

We know it sounds cliché, but our all-time favorite side dish recipe in this book is the Crispy Roasted Potatoes (page 171). They are super versatile, you can serve them with anything, and they taste fabulous too. If you are planning a fancy dinner or really want to impress, definitely don't skip the Melted Camembert Cheese with Garlic Crostini (page 179). If you are more of a planner, then the Marinated Roasted Vegetables (page 182)—our method for antipasti—is for you. You can make them up to 7 days ahead, so there will be zero stress the day of the party.

ROASTED CARROTS
with Honey

SERVES 4

PREP TIME: 5 minutes

ROASTING TIME:
20–25 minutes

CARROTS

1 lb (450 g) small carrots, cut into
1-inch (2-cm) diagonal chunks

4 tbsp (56 g) unsalted butter

2 cloves garlic, diced

1 tbsp (15 ml) honey

1 tbsp (15 ml) white wine vinegar or
rice vinegar

¼ cup (60 ml) freshly squeezed orange
juice or water

Salt and freshly ground black pepper

FOR SERVING

Freshly grated lime zest
Freshly squeezed lime juice
Grated fresh red chile, such as serrano

Roasted carrots and honey: such a sweet combination. I would serve this simple homemade side dish for all cold-weather holidays. They are hearty, comforting, and incredibly delicious. The carrots are roasted in orange juice, white wine vinegar, honey, and garlic, which helps them develop even sweeter flavor and juiciness. They are soft and tasty, while still having that beautifully roasted exterior.

Arrange a rack in the middle of the oven, then preheat it to 450°F (230°C).

Spread the carrots in a single layer in a deep baking dish.

Melt the butter in a saucepan over medium-low heat. Add the garlic, and cook it for 1 minute, then add the honey, vinegar, and orange juice. Bring the mixture to a boil, then pour it over the carrots. Season with salt and pepper.

Roast the carrots on the middle rack of the oven for 20 to 25 minutes, or until the carrots are glazed, shiny, and tender when tested with a knife.

To serve, sprinkle the carrots with the lime zest, lime juice, and chile.

SWEET POTATO FRIES

SERVES 4

PREP TIME: 10 minutes

ROASTING TIME:
15 minutes

FRIES
2 lbs (900 g) sweet potatoes, cut into
½-inch (1-cm)-thick fries
2 tbsp (30 ml) canola oil
½ tsp freshly ground black pepper or
to taste
½ tsp smoked paprika or to taste
¼ tsp ground coriander
Salt

FOR SERVING
Roasted Garlic and Lemon Mayonnaise
(page 231) or ketchup

Usually, fries would be fried. But in this case, they are roasted in the oven for a short time, which makes them a delicious side for any day of the week. They aren't as crispy as fried potatoes would be, but the flavor is not compromised at all. Our seasoning mixture makes the sweet potatoes slightly spiced and flavorful, but the spices don't overtake the flavor of the sweet, earthy potatoes. Our Roasted Garlic and Lemon Mayonnaise (page 231) complements the sweet potatoes beautifully.

Arrange a rack in the middle of the oven, then preheat it to 450°F (230°C). Place a wire rack in a baking sheet.

Place the sweet potato fries on a large plate or tray. Season them with the oil, pepper, smoked paprika, and coriander. Toss everything together to combine it.

Arrange the sweet potato fries over the prepared wire rack in a single layer. Roast the sweet potatoes for 15 minutes, or until they are tender and golden brown.

Sprinkle the sweet potato fries with salt and serve immediately with the mayonnaise. These are best when fresh.

ROASTED ROOT VEGETABLES

SERVES 4

PREP TIME: 5 minutes

ROASTING TIME:
20–25 minutes

Roasted root vegetables are sweet, tender, and can keep you full for hours, especially if you stir them into cooked couscous or quinoa and serve them with a generous dollop of Greek yogurt, as we do. This makes the perfect side for roasted meat or can even make a simple, yet incredibly tasty, vegetarian dinner. Choose your favorite root vegetables, and be sure to cut them into small chunks, because we want them cooked in less than 30 minutes.

ROOT VEGETABLES

2 lbs (900 g) root vegetables, such as carrots, parsnips, rutabagas, onions, or beets, cut into ½-inch (1-cm) cubes

Salt and freshly ground black pepper

1 tsp dried thyme

2 tbsp (30 ml) melted unsalted butter

1 tbsp (15 ml) balsamic vinegar

1 tbsp (15 ml) canola or olive oil

FOR SERVING

1 tbsp (5 g) chopped fresh parsley

1 tbsp (5 g) chopped fresh mint

Cooked couscous or quinoa, optional

Greek yogurt, optional

Arrange a rack in the middle of the oven, then preheat the oven to 450°F (230°C).

Place the root vegetables in a single layer on a baking sheet. Season the vegetables generously with salt and pepper; add the thyme. Drizzle the butter, vinegar, and oil over the vegetables, and toss together to combine.

Roast the vegetables for 20 to 25 minutes, or until they are tender when tested with a knife. Stir the vegetables halfway through the roasting time.

For serving, remove the root vegetables from the oven. Season them to taste with salt, then sprinkle the parsley and mint. Serve the vegetables as a side, or stir them into the couscous, if using, and spoon a generous dollop of the yogurt, if using, on top for a main dish.

CRISPY ROASTED POTATOES

SERVES 4

PREP TIME: 10 minutes

ROASTING TIME:
18–20 minutes

2 lbs (900 g) potatoes, unpeeled and cut into 1-inch (2-cm) chunks
2 tbsp (30 ml) olive oil
1 tbsp (6 g) breadcrumbs
Salt

Say hello to your next favorite side dish. Most of the people we know love crispy, roasted potatoes. The crunchy, golden-brown exterior and soft, delicious interior make for a beautiful combination of textures that can be achieved with just a little time and effort. We sprinkle the potatoes with breadcrumbs to give them some extra crunchiness and texture, while the flavor stays super tasty. Serve these as a snack or side any day of the year.

Arrange a rack at the top of the oven, then preheat it to 480°F (250°C). Grease a baking sheet.

Bring a pot of salted water to a boil over medium-high heat. Add the potatoes, and cook them for 6 to 8 minutes, or until they are just slightly cooked. Drain the potatoes in a colander, then let them stand in the colander for 2 minutes; this step releases steam, prevents sogginess, and ensures crunchiness.

Place the potatoes on the prepared baking sheet. Drizzle them with the oil, add the breadcrumbs, and toss to combine the ingredients. Roast the potatoes on the top rack of the oven for 13 to 15 minutes, until they are crisp-tender. Stir the potatoes once while roasting. Then, change the temperature to high broil, and broil the potatoes for 5 minutes, or until they are crispy and golden brown.

Remove the potatoes from the oven, sprinkle them with salt, and serve.

NOTE: Cut the potatoes as uniformly as possible, so that they roast evenly.

CRISPY PORK CRACKLING

SERVES 4

PREP TIME: 2 minutes

ROASTING TIME:
20–25 minutes

½ lb (225 g) pork rind
Salt

Instead of chips, serve this homemade pork crackling at your next party. The mouthwatering, super-crispy, and delicious crackling is made from two simple ingredients: pork rind and salt. This simple pork snack keeps, in an airtight container at room temperature, for up to a week.

Arrange a rack in the middle of the oven, then preheat it to 450°F (230°C). Put a wire rack in a baking sheet.

Using a sharp knife or a box cutter, make a few parallel shallow cuts into the skin of the pork rind. Don't go through the skin. Then, make a few shallow cuts in the other direction, making a diamond pattern; this prevents the pork rind from curling up.

Place the pork rind, skin side up, on the prepared rack. Roast the pork rind on the middle rack of the oven for 20 to 25 minutes, or until the rind is crispy and bubbles appear on top.

Remove the pork rind from the oven, and let it cool for a few minutes. Chop the pork rind into chip-sized pieces, then season them with salt.

SPICED ROASTED PEPITAS

SERVES 4

PREP TIME: 10 minutes

ROASTING TIME:
8–10 minutes

½ lb (225 g) pepitas
1 tsp olive oil
1 tsp paprika
¼ tsp smoked paprika
½ tsp dried oregano
Salt
¼ tsp garlic powder

When I (Maja) was a kid, my dad and I used to visit the farmers' market every other Saturday. An older woman there sold only two things: pepitas and salted, roasted whole pumpkin seeds. To me, that was the best snack I could get. My dad would always buy a small bag of each treat for me, and I was just the happiest kid alive. To this day, more than twenty years later, the same woman sells from that same farmers' market. We bought the pepitas for this recipe from her. These are the easiest, healthiest snack you can make at home. They are crunchy, spicy, and all-natural. We always have them in the pantry for ourselves and for our friends, too.

Arrange a rack in the middle of the oven, then preheat it to 390°F (200°C).

On a baking sheet, drizzle the pepitas with the oil, and then season with the paprika, smoked paprika, oregano, salt, and garlic powder. Toss to combine the ingredients.

Roast the pepitas on the middle rack of the oven for 8 to 10 minutes, or until the pepitas have turned golden brown and crunchy.

Transfer the roasted pepitas to a bowl to cool, then serve them. The pepitas can be stored at room temperature, in an airtight container, for up to 14 days.

CHICKPEAS
with Paprika

SERVES 4

PREP TIME: 2 minutes

ROASTING TIME:
20–30 minutes

2 (15-oz [425-g]) cans cooked
chickpeas, drained
1 tsp Spanish smoked paprika
1 tbsp (5 g) paprika
2 tbsp (30 ml) olive oil
1 tsp freshly grated lemon zest
Salt and freshly ground black pepper

Roasted chickpeas with paprika is a snack that we just love to have around the house at all times. Chickpeas are a great source of protein and make a healthy snack. Sure, you can go the extra mile and cook the chickpeas at home, but since this is a cookbook of 30-minute recipes, we decided to use canned chickpeas. Make sure to drain them well before roasting them, and be generous with the seasoning. The better the quality of the paprika, the better the aroma during roasting.

Arrange a rack in the middle of the oven, then preheat it to 430°F (220°C).

Arrange the chickpeas over two layers of paper towels. Pat the chickpeas dry with another paper towel. Spread the chickpeas on a baking sheet in a single layer. Season them with the smoked paprika, paprika, and oil; toss to combine.

Roast the chickpeas on the middle rack of the oven for 20 minutes, or until they are dry and crispy on the outside and soft inside. Toss the chickpeas from time to time while they are roasting. If you want extra-crunchy chickpeas, roast them for an additional 5 to 10 minutes, but be sure to keep an eye on them.

Remove the chickpeas from the oven. While they are still hot, season them with the lemon zest and salt and pepper. Toss to coat, transfer to a bowl, and serve. The chickpeas keep, in an airtight container at room temperature, for up to 3 days.

MELTED CAMEMBERT CHEESE

with Garlic Crostini

SERVES 4

PREP TIME: 5 minutes

ROASTING TIME: 15–18 minutes

CROSTINI

½ French baguette, cut into ½-inch (1-cm) slices

2 tbsp (30 ml) olive oil

1 clove garlic, minced

ROASTED CAMEMBERT

1 (8½–10½-oz [240–300-g]) Camembert cheese

1 tsp olive oil

¼ tsp freshly ground black pepper

FOR SERVING

½ tsp chopped fresh thyme

Chopped pistachios

Honey

Roasted Camembert is such a fancy snack or appetizer. The cheese comes in a wooden box, and it remains in that box while roasting; just be sure to remove all the plastic. Roasting this type of cheese is magnificent. It becomes super gooey and melted, and it begs you to dig in. Grilled bread or homemade garlic crostini is essential to have on hand, because, believe me, no one can resist roasted Camembert. The cheese has a deep, earthy, specific flavor, so it is good to accompany it with a drizzle of honey for sweetness and some chopped pistachios for crunchiness. It also pairs well with onion marmalade or chutney.

Arrange racks at the top of and in the middle of the oven, then preheat the oven to 410°F (210°C). Line a baking sheet with parchment paper.

For the crostini, place the baguette slices in a single layer on a large baking sheet. In a small bowl, stir to combine the oil and garlic. Brush the crostini on both sides with the mixture. Roast the crostini on the top rack of the oven for 3 minutes, or until the bread is golden and crunchy.

For the Camembert, remove the plastic packaging from the cheese. Leave the cheese in its wooden box; leave off the lid. Pierce the top of the cheese several times using a sharp knife. Drizzle it with the olive oil, and season with the pepper. Place the cheese on the prepared baking sheet, and roast it on the middle rack of the oven for 12 to 15 minutes, or until the cheese is melted.

To serve, sprinkle the Camembert with the thyme and pistachios, drizzle it with honey, and serve it immediately with the crostini for dipping.

BALSAMIC-ROASTED FIGS
with Parmesan Crisp

SERVES 4

PREP TIME: 5 minutes

ROASTING TIME:
14–18 minutes

PARMESAN CRISP
1 cup (100 g) finely grated Parmesan cheese

FIGS
8 figs
Salt and freshly ground black pepper
1 tbsp (15 ml) olive oil
2 tbsp (30 ml) balsamic vinegar
1 tsp honey

FOR SERVING
Olives
Bread
Salami
Prosciutto

Get the juiciest summer figs you can for this simple appetizer or snack. I can hardly stop eating fresh figs picked straight from the tree; they offer much-needed refreshment in the summer. Roasted figs are just the juiciest, sweetest thing you will ever eat. They are beautifully caramelized with balsamic vinegar and honey and served with a side of thin Parmesan crisp, which adds saltiness and a melted-cheese flavor that is just marvelous. These figs make a luxurious snack or appetizer, prepared in minutes with little effort. When we serve the figs as an appetizer, we add a selection of cheeses and salami. The richness of the meat and cheese contrasts with the sweetness of the figs.

Arrange a rack in the middle of the oven, then preheat it to 450°F (230°C). Line a baking sheet with parchment paper. Line a wire rack with paper towels.

For the Parmesan crisp, spread the Parmesan cheese in a single layer on the prepared baking sheet. Roast the cheese on the middle rack of the oven for 6 to 8 minutes, or until it's golden brown (see Note).

While the Parmesan is roasting, cut the figs in half, and season them with salt and pepper. Place them, cut side down, on a separate baking sheet. Drizzle them with the oil, vinegar, and honey.

Remove the cheese from the oven, and transfer it to the prepared rack. Set it aside to cool completely.

Change the oven temperature to 410°F (210°C). Roast the figs on the middle rack of the oven for 8 to 10 minutes, or until they are soft and juicy.

To serve, arrange the figs on a serving platter with olives, bread, salami, and prosciutto. Break the cheese into smaller pieces to eat with the figs.

NOTE: Feel free to make the Parmesan crisp up to 2 days in advance. Store it in an airtight container at room temperature.

MARINATED ROASTED VEGETABLES

SERVES 4-6

PREP TIME: 5 minutes

ROASTING TIME:
15–25 minutes

Preserving vegetables in this way is easy and quick. It allows us always to have roasted peppers, eggplant, cherry tomatoes, or zucchini on hand for antipasti, when we expect friends over, or when we crave something extra with our favorite selection of cheese and salami. This recipe includes a simple antipasto dressing that you can use for all kinds of vegetables, not just for our four favorites, which we included here. You can refrigerate the vegetables, stored in an airtight container, for up to 7 days.

MARINADE

4 cloves garlic, diced

1 handful parsley, chopped

¼ cup (60 ml) olive oil

¼ cup (60 ml) canola oil

1 tbsp (15 ml) sherry vinegar or balsamic vinegar

Salt and freshly ground black pepper

For the marinade, in a bowl, stir together the garlic, parsley, olive oil, canola oil, and vinegar. Season with salt and pepper, and use the dressing with one of the following recipes.

ROASTED PEPPERS

4 Italian long sweet red peppers or red bell peppers

ROASTED PEPPERS

Arrange a rack at the top of the oven, then preheat the oven to high broil.

Place the peppers on a baking sheet. Broil the peppers on the top rack of the oven for 12 minutes, then turn them. Roast for 8 minutes, or until they are completely blackened outside and soft inside.

Remove the roasted peppers from the oven. Place them in a freezer bag for 5 minutes, to stem them and make them easier to peel. Remove the peppers from the bag. Rub the skins off the peppers using paper towels. Cut the roasted peppers lengthwise, and scrape out the seeds.

Spoon the marinade over the roasted peppers and serve.

ROASTED EGGPLANT

1 eggplant, cut into 1-inch (2-cm) rings

1 tbsp (15 ml) olive oil

Salt and freshly ground black pepper

ROASTED CHERRY TOMATOES

1 lb (450 g) cherry tomatoes on the vine

1 tbsp (15 ml) olive oil

Salt and freshly ground black pepper

ROASTED ZUCCHINI

2 zucchinis, quartered lengthwise and cut into 3-inch (8-cm) pieces

1 tbsp (15 ml) olive oil

ROASTED EGGPLANT

Arrange a rack in the middle of the oven, then preheat it to 450°F (230°C).

Cut a ¼-inch (½-cm) crisscross pattern into the skin of each eggplant ring; scoring the flesh this way allows it to roast evenly. Place the rings on a baking sheet, drizzle them with the oil, and season them with salt and pepper.

Roast the eggplant for 25 minutes, or until the eggplant is soft when tested with a knife. Turn the eggplant halfway through the roasting time.

Spoon the marinade over the roasted eggplant and serve.

ROASTED CHERRY TOMATOES

Arrange a rack in the middle of the oven, then preheat it to 450°F (230°C).

Place the tomatoes on a baking sheet, drizzle them with the oil, and season them with salt and pepper. Roast the tomatoes for 25 minutes, or until they are juicy and slightly charred.

Transfer the tomatoes to a serving platter. Pour the roasting juices over the tomatoes. Drizzle them with the marinade and serve.

ROASTED ZUCCHINI

Arrange a rack in the middle of the oven, then preheat it to 450°F (230°C).

Place the zucchini on a baking sheet, and drizzle it with the oil. Toss everything together, so that every piece is nicely coated with oil.

Roast the zucchini on the middle rack of the oven for 15 to 20 minutes, or until it's soft when tested with a knife. Drizzle the zucchini with the marinade and serve.

*See photo on page 162.

IT'S BRUNCH O'CLOCK

We love brunch. The recipes in this chapter are incredibly easy to make, and they will keep you full until late lunch or even dinner.

Here, in this chapter, you will find our two all-time favorite crostini recipes: Sourdough with Roasted Grapes, Cream Cheese, and Honey (page 186) and Roasted Tomato Crostini with Basil Pesto (page 193). These are incredibly full of flavor and easy to make. Our favorite soup recipe in this chapter is Roasted Cherry Tomato Soup with Garlic Bread (page 198). It is light, delicious, and naturally sweet, plus it keeps you full for hours—the perfect little brunch treat.

SOURDOUGH
with Roasted Grapes, Cream Cheese, and Honey

SERVES 4

PREP TIME: 10 minutes

ROASTING TIME: 10–15 minutes

ROASTED GRAPES

1 lb (450 g) seedless red grapes

1 tbsp (15 ml) olive oil

1 tbsp (15 ml) floral honey

1 tsp balsamic vinegar

Salt and freshly ground black pepper

FOR SERVING

4 slices sourdough bread

⅔ cup (150 g) cream cheese

1 tbsp (15 ml) olive oil

1 tbsp (15 ml) honey

Pinch of salt

1 tbsp (5 g) chopped fresh oregano

1 tbsp (5 g) chopped fresh rosemary

1 handful walnuts or pecans, chopped

This simple appetizer quickly became a staple and a family favorite. Maja's mom was especially skeptical about the flavor combination at first, but her facial expression pure joy, happiness, and excitement—after trying the first bite was something I will cherish forever. That look is exactly what you want to see on people's faces when you serve them homemade goods. The biggest tip for success with this recipe is to get the best possible sourdough bread, extra-creamy cream cheese, and good floral honey. Don't forget a pinch of salt at the end; it makes all the difference. Feel free to serve this warm or cold for breakfast, brunch, or an appetizer.

Arrange a rack in the middle of the oven, then preheat it to 410°F (210°C).

Place the grapes on a baking sheet. Drizzle them with the oil, honey, and vinegar. Season with salt and pepper. Roast the grapes on the middle rack of the oven for 10 to 15 minutes, or until they are juicy and tender.

To serve, toast the sourdough bread and spread a generous amount of cream cheese on top. Add 2 tablespoons (50 g) of roasted grapes to each slice. Drizzle the grapes with the oil and honey, and sprinkle the crostini with the salt, oregano, rosemary, and walnuts.

OATMEAL
with Roasted Apple and Blueberries

SERVES 4

PREP TIME: 5 minutes

ROASTING TIME:
18–20 minutes

ROASTED APPLES AND BLUEBERRIES

4 tbsp (60 ml) melted unsalted butter

4 large apples, cored, peeled, and cut into wedges

4 tbsp (60 g) brown sugar

2 tbsp (30 ml) freshly squeezed lemon juice

2 tbsp (30 ml) honey

1 tsp ground cinnamon

1 tbsp (8 g) cornstarch

¼ cup (60 ml) water

2 cups (300 g) blueberries

OATMEAL

4 cups (400 g) old-fashioned oats

4 cups (960 ml) water

4 cups (960 ml) oat milk

¼ tsp salt

FOR SERVING

Chopped pecans, optional

Maple syrup, optional

If you are looking for a quick and delicious breakfast or brunch recipe that is full of flavor, then you just hit the jackpot. First, we roast apples and blueberries along with cinnamon, brown sugar, and honey, and, while the fruits are roasting, we make creamy and delicious oatmeal. It's a beautiful dish that can be served warm or cold, for a quick brunch on the go or a luxurious weekend breakfast.

Arrange a rack in the middle of the oven, then preheat it to 430°F (220°C).

For the roasted fruit, in a large bowl, pour the butter over the apples. Add the brown sugar, lemon juice, honey, cinnamon, cornstarch, and water. Stir to combine. Add the blueberries, stir, and put the fruit on a baking sheet. Roast the fruit on the middle rack of the oven for 18 to 20 minutes, or until it's juicy and soft.

While the fruit is roasting, make the oatmeal. In a saucepan, combine the old-fashioned oats, water, oat milk, and salt. Bring the mixture to a boil over medium-high heat, then cook it on low simmer for 2 to 3 minutes. Remove the oatmeal from the heat, cover the pan with a lid, and let the oatmeal sit for 5 minutes.

To serve, spoon the cooked oatmeal into your favorite breakfast bowls. Top it with the roasted apples and blueberries. Top the fruit with the pecans and maple syrup, if using.

ROASTED PEPPERS AND ITALIAN PORK SAUSAGES

SERVES 4

PREP TIME: 5 minutes

ROASTING TIME:
23–25 minutes

This is such a colorful summertime roast that celebrates bell peppers and pork sausages. We serve this simple dish for a picnic often. You can easily prepare everything in advance, then pop it in the oven right before serving. It is so easy and so quick to make. The vegetables are beautifully caramelized, naturally sweet, and crunchy, while the pork sausages get perfectly cooked through with a golden-brown, roasted exterior.

ROASTED PEPPERS AND SAUSAGES

3 colorful bell peppers, stemmed, seeded, and cut into chunks

4 Italian pork sausages, cut into 1-inch (2-cm) slices

2 shallots, quartered

1 clove garlic, cut in half

6 cherry tomatoes, cut in half

1 tbsp (15 ml) olive oil

Salt and freshly ground black pepper

1 sprig fresh thyme

12 olives

FOR SERVING

Chopped fresh herbs, optional

Turkish Roasted Red Pepper Dip (page 235)

Italian ciabatta bread or French baguette

Arrange racks in the middle and at the top of the oven, then preheat it to 450°F (230°C).

For the peppers and sausages, put the peppers, sausages, shallots, garlic, and cherry tomatoes in a deep, broiler-safe baking dish. Drizzle the olive oil, season with salt and pepper, and add the thyme. Toss to combine.

Roast the sausages and peppers on the middle rack of the oven for 15 minutes.

Remove the dish from the oven, and sprinkle the olives on top. Change the oven temperature to low broil, and return the dish to the oven, on the top rack. Broil the sausages and peppers for 8 to 10 minutes, or until the sausages are crispy and the peppers are soft. Stir the sausages and peppers a couple of times while broiling.

To serve, sprinkle the dish with the herbs, if using, and serve it with the dip and bread.

ROASTED TOMATO CROSTINI

with Basil Pesto

SERVES 4

PREP TIME: 10 minutes

ROASTING TIME:
20–25 minutes

ROASTED CHERRY TOMATOES

½ lb (225 g) cherry tomatoes on the vine

1 tbsp (15 ml) olive oil

Salt and freshly ground black pepper

BASIL PESTO

1 handful fresh basil leaves

2 tbsp (12 g) freshly grated Parmesan cheese

1 tsp breadcrumbs

3 tbsp (45 ml) olive oil

1 tbsp (10 g) blanched almonds

Salt

FOR SERVING

4 slices sourdough bread

3 tbsp (45 g) cream cheese

Roasted cherry tomato crostini are right for breakfast, brunch, an appetizer, or even a light midweek lunch. They are our go-to summer snack, packed with flavor and juiciness. Roast cherry tomatoes on the vine to get the best flavor. This roasting technique can be used for all kinds of dishes, such as Roasted Cherry Tomato Soup with Garlic Bread (page 198). Add roasted cherry tomatoes to pasta and salads, or eat them plain. Not only do basil and tomatoes grow together and complement each other in the garden, but their tastes also complement each other beautifully. Sweet, roasted tomatoes, and fresh, herby basil pesto is an impressive, fantastic, classic combination.

Arrange a rack in the middle of the oven, then preheat it to 450°F (230°C).

For the roasted tomatoes, put the vine of cherry tomatoes on a baking sheet. Drizzle the oil over the tomatoes, and season them with salt and pepper. Roast the tomatoes on the middle rack of the oven for 20 to 25 minutes, or until they are juicy and slightly charred.

While the tomatoes are roasting, make the basil pesto. In a food processor, pulse the basil, Parmesan, breadcrumbs, oil, and almonds to get a smooth pesto. Season to taste with salt. If the pesto is too thick, add 1 tablespoon (15 ml) of water and pulse the mixture again.

To serve, toast the bread, and spread it with a generous amount of cream cheese. Add four roasted cherry tomatoes on top of each slice, top with the pesto, and serve.

NOTE: The basil pesto can be refrigerated for up to 3 days. To prevent oxidation, keep it in the dark by completely covering it with aluminum foil.

SIMPLE ROASTED CAULIFLOWER SOUP

SERVES 4

PREP TIME: 5 minutes

ROASTING TIME:
20 minutes

Roasted cauliflower soup is one of our favorite warming soups. It is creamy, hearty, and healthy. Roasting the cauliflower in the oven instead of cooking it on the stove helps develop a lot of flavor and character. Instead of being boring and bland, this soup is infused with garlic, nutmeg, and, of course, roasted cauliflower flavor. Serve this soup for lunch or a light dinner.

Arrange a rack in the middle of the oven, then preheat it to 450°F (230°C).

For the soup, arrange the cauliflower florets in a single layer on a baking sheet. Add the onion and garlic, and season with salt and pepper. Drizzle the vegetables with the butter and oil. Toss to combine.

Roast the vegetables on the middle rack of the oven for 20 minutes, or until they are soft when tested with a knife.

In a soup pot, bring the milk, stock, nutmeg, and bay leaf to a boil over medium-high heat.

Remove the roasted cauliflower mixture from the oven and transfer it to a blender. Add half of the milk mixture and blend. Use caution when blending hot liquids. After a couple of minutes of mixing, add the rest of the milk mixture, and blend it into a creamy, smooth soup. Add the lemon juice, and season to taste with salt and pepper.

To serve, ladle the soup into four bowls. Top each serving with a spoonful of sour cream, parsley, a drizzle of olive oil, fresh oregano, and nuts, if using. Serve with the crostini.

SOUP

1 head cauliflower, cut into small florets

½ onion, cut into quarters

1 clove garlic, crushed

Salt and freshly ground black pepper

4 tbsp (60 ml) melted unsalted butter

1 tbsp (15 ml) olive oil

2 cups (480 ml) milk

1 cup (240 ml) chicken stock or water

½ tsp freshly grated nutmeg

1 bay leaf

1 tsp freshly squeezed lemon juice

Salt and freshly ground black pepper

FOR SERVING

Sour cream, optional

Chopped fresh parsley, optional

Olive oil, optional

Chopped fresh oregano, optional

Chopped walnuts or pecans, optional

Grilled crostini

ROASTED BUTTERNUT SQUASH SOUP

SERVES 4

PREP TIME: 5 minutes

ROASTING TIME:
20–25 minutes

SOUP

1½ lbs (680 g) butternut squash, cut
into ½-inch (1-cm) cubes (see Note)

1 shallot, chopped

1 onion, chopped

2 cloves garlic, crushed

2 tbsp (30 ml) olive oil

½ tsp salt

½ tsp freshly ground black pepper

½ tsp ground nutmeg

½ cup (120 ml) heavy cream

2–2½ cups (480–600 ml) water

FOR SERVING

Spiced Roasted Pepitas (page 175),
optional

4 tsp (20 ml) heavy cream

Butternut squash soup must be one of the comfiest, coziest soups. It's thick, creamy, and naturally slightly sweet, especially when the squash is oven-roasted. This soup is made in minutes, and it makes the most delicious light, homemade lunch for cold autumn and winter days. It is fancy and beautiful enough to serve for special occasions, such as winter holidays and date-night dinners. This soup will warm your body and soul, and you won't be able to get enough of it. If you have the time, we recommend making Spiced Roasted Pepitas (page 175) to serve with the soup, to add extra flavor and crunch.

Arrange a rack in the middle of the oven, then preheat it to 450°F (230°C).

For the soup, arrange the squash in a single layer on a baking sheet. Add the shallot, onion, and garlic. Drizzle the vegetables with the oil, and season them with the salt, pepper, and nutmeg.

Roast the vegetables on the middle rack of the oven for 20 to 25 minutes, or until they are soft when tested with a knife and caramelized.

In a soup pot, bring the cream and water to a boil over medium-high heat. Add the roasted butternut squash mixture, and blend it into a creamy soup using an immersion blender.

To serve, ladle the soup into four bowls, then sprinkle it with the pepitas, if using. Top the soup with a teaspoon of heavy cream.

NOTE: The smaller the butternut squash cubes, the faster the roasting time. Small squash cubes also develop more flavor from caramelization.

ROASTED CHERRY TOMATO SOUP

with Garlic Bread

SERVES 4

PREP TIME: 5 minutes

ROASTING TIME:
18–25 minutes

SOUP

1½ lbs (680 g) cherry tomatoes

3 cloves garlic, smashed

1 tbsp (15 g) sugar, optional

1 tbsp (15 ml) olive oil, plus more for drizzling

1 tsp balsamic vinegar

Salt and freshly ground black pepper

1 bunch fresh basil

1 cup (240 ml) boiling water

GARLIC BREAD

½ French baguette

2 cloves garlic, minced

2 tbsp (30 ml) olive oil

1 tbsp chopped fresh parsley

In our garden, cherry tomatoes are always growing in such abundance that it's nice to have different ways to use them. Besides enjoying them as a homegrown snack or in a salad with mozzarella cheese, olive oil, and fresh basil, we love roasted cherry tomato soup. Sure, you could use any other variety of tomatoes, but cherry tomatoes are the way to go if you are short on time, because they roast faster and they are much sweeter than other tomatoes. This cherry tomato soup is a beautiful, flavorful summer and early-autumn soup that's incredibly easy to make. Serve it for brunch or lunch with our crusty, aromatic garlic bread.

Arrange racks in the middle and at the bottom of the oven, then preheat it to 450°F (230°C).

Add the tomatoes, garlic, and sugar, if using, to a baking sheet. Drizzle the vegetables with the oil and vinegar, and season with salt and pepper. Toss to combine the ingredients.

Roast the tomatoes on the middle rack of the oven for 15 to 20 minutes, or until they are juicy and bursting.

Meanwhile, prepare the garlic bread. Cut the loaf almost all the way through into 1-inch (2-cm)-thick slices. In a bowl, stir to combine the garlic, oil, and parsley. Pour the mixture over the bread, and smear it over the cut side of the bread. On a small baking sheet, roast the bread on the lower rack of the oven for 3 to 5 minutes, or until it's golden brown and crispy.

Remove the roasted tomatoes from the oven. Using a blender or a food processor, blend or pulse the tomato mixture, roasting juices, basil, and hot water until the mixture is smooth. Use caution when blending hot liquids. If necessary, thin the soup with additional water.

Serve the soup with a drizzle of olive oil and the garlic bread.

ZUCCHINI
with Sun-Dried Tomato Pesto and Burrata

SERVES 4

PREP TIME: 5 minutes

ROASTING TIME:
15–18 minutes

ROASTED ZUCCHINI

1½ lbs (680 g) zucchini, cut in half lengthwise, then into 2-inch (4-cm) chunks

1 tbsp (15 ml) olive oil

Salt and freshly ground black pepper

½ tsp dried oregano

SUN-DRIED TOMATO PESTO

⅓ cup (18 g) sun-dried tomatoes

¼ cup (60 ml) olive oil

1 tbsp (15 ml) freshly squeezed lemon juice

1 clove garlic, diced

¼ cup (40 g) pine nuts

¼ cup (20 g) sliced almonds

Salt and freshly ground black pepper

½ tsp oregano

Pinch of crushed red pepper

FOR SERVING

3½ oz (100 g) burrata cheese

1 tbsp (5 g) chopped fresh parsley

Olive oil

Pine nuts, optional

We really need to get creative with zucchini in the summer. There is no stopping them when they are in season. The garden is full of zucchini, and they keep growing for months. So, we need to keep finding new ways to use them. This oregano-flavored roasted zucchini, topped with a simple, homemade sun-dried tomato pesto, is just unreal. It screams summer, and these roasted zucchinis make the perfect healthy, vegetarian summer appetizer or brunch salad. The pesto is bursting with flavor, and the burrata adds a much-needed fresh balance to the whole dish. For some extra flavor, drizzle the dish with high-quality olive oil.

Arrange a rack in the middle of the oven, then preheat it to 450°F (230°C).

Spread the zucchini over a baking sheet in a single layer. Drizzle it with the oil. Season it with salt and pepper, add the oregano, then toss to combine the ingredients.

Roast the zucchini on the middle rack of the oven for 15 to 18 minutes, or until it is soft when tested with a knife.

While the zucchini is roasting, make the sun-dried tomato pesto. In a bowl, combine the tomatoes, oil, lemon juice, garlic, pine nuts, and almonds. Using an immersion blender, blend the mixture into a pesto. Add up to 2 tablespoons (30 ml) of water, if needed, to thin the pesto, then blend again. Season to taste with salt and pepper, then add the oregano and crushed red pepper. Stir and set aside.

To serve, remove the zucchini from the oven. Transfer it to a serving platter. Spoon the sun-dried tomato pesto over the zucchini. Tear the burrata, and put the pieces on top of the pesto. Sprinkle the cheese with the parsley, and drizzle it with the oil. Top with the pine nuts, if using.

HANDS-OFF SWEET TREATS

When you think of roasts, the first thing that probably comes to mind is meat, vegetables, or fish. However, roasting fruits can translate to many incredibly delicious, sweet, and simple desserts that are flavorful and irresistible. Stone fruits are known for roasting beautifully, as is pineapple. But the biggest challenge was to make a chocolate cake and cheesecake that could be baked at high temperature in under 30 minutes.

The solution for chocolate cake is to bake it in small ramekins. All of you chocolate lovers: Give Speedy Soft Dark Chocolate Cake (page 220) a go. It's super soft, fluffy, and intensely chocolaty. For a quick and super-easy summertime afternoon dessert, make Roasted Berries Sundae (page 212). You combine roasted berries with the best-quality vanilla ice cream and dig in. Our favorite wintertime dessert must be Roasted Apples with Cornflakes (page 204), which tastes like apple pie but is much faster and easier to prepare. For a sweet snack on the go, make the Salted Caramel Nuts (page 223), which every kid and adult loves.

Choose a quick and easy dessert to serve after enjoying a beautiful main dish roast from this book. The oven is already hot and running.

ROASTED APPLES
with Cornflakes

SERVES 4

PREP TIME: 5 minutes

ROASTING TIME:
25 minutes

ROASTED APPLES

4 Braeburn apples, cored, peeled, and
cut into wedges

3 tbsp (45 g) packed light brown sugar

1 tsp ground cinnamon

½ tsp ground ginger

1 tsp cornstarch

½ tsp vanilla bean paste

2 tbsp (30 ml) melted unsalted butter

CRUMBLE

2 cups (50 g) cornflakes

2 tbsp (18 g) all-purpose flour

Pinch of salt

4 tbsp (60 g) sugar

4 tbsp (60 g) cold unsalted butter

FOR SERVING

Vanilla bean ice cream

Would you believe me if I said that Roasted Apples with Cornflakes tastes like apple pie? It does. It tastes like the best apple pie you have ever eaten. Beautifully caramelized and spiced apple wedges are covered with a cornflake crumble that creates the crunchiest, crumbliest, golden-brown topping. And, what makes it all even better is the fact that this dessert is made in less than 30 minutes. Add a generous scoop of ice cream to make this dessert even better. This is perfect for holidays, birthday gatherings, or a quick dessert during a week when you need something comforting and easily prepared at home.

Arrange a rack in the middle of the oven, then preheat it to 450°F (230°C).

Place the apples in a deep baking dish, and sprinkle them with the brown sugar, cinnamon, ginger, and cornstarch. Add the vanilla bean paste and the butter. Rub the ingredients into the apples.

Roast the apples on the middle rack of the oven for 15 minutes.

Make the crumble while the apples roast. In a large bowl, crush the cornflakes into small pieces with your hands. Add the flour, salt, and sugar. Using your fingertips, lightly rub the butter into the mixture, until you get a delicate crumb. Set aside the mixture.

When the apples have roasted for 15 minutes, remove them from the oven. Reduce the oven temperature to 410°F (210°C). Spread the crumble on top of the apples, then roast them for 10 minutes, or until the crumble is golden brown and crisp and the apples are bubbling and tender.

To serve, divide the roasted apples among four plates. Top with a generous scoop of the ice cream and serve.

ULTIMATE "BURNT" BASQUE CHEESECAKE POTS

SERVES 4

PREP TIME: 5 minutes

ROASTING TIME:
20 minutes

CHEESECAKE

1⅓ cups (300 g) cream cheese

2 eggs

½ cup (120 g) sugar

1 cup (240 ml) heavy cream

1 tsp vanilla extract

½ tsp salt

2 tbsp (18 g) all-purpose flour

FOR SERVING

Fresh berries

These mini cheesecake pots are a showstopper. Don't let the word "burnt" scare you. They look like we baked them for far too long, but, in reality, they are incredibly creamy and soft. This Spanish cheesecake got its name from the dark, caramelized, cracked top. Instead of baking it longer, at a lower temperature, we roast this cheesecake at a high temperature for a shorter time. The interior is perfectly cooked through, fluffy, and delicious. Using small ramekins instead of a large pie dish highly reduces the cooking time, but we still get the same result and flavor.

Arrange a rack in the middle of the oven, then preheat it to 430°F (220°C). Place four broiler-proof 4-inch (10-cm) ramekins on a baking sheet.

For the cheesecake, combine the cream cheese, eggs, sugar, cream, vanilla, salt, and flour in a food processor. Mix for about 2 minutes, until the mixture is silky smooth and creamy.

Evenly spoon the batter into the ramekins. Roast the cheesecake on the middle rack of the oven for 18 minutes. Then, increase the temperature to high broil for 2 minutes, or until the cakes are dark brown—the signature burnt look—but still slightly jiggly in the center.

To serve, let the cheesecakes cool slightly, then top them with the berries.

NOTE: Use cast-iron or ceramic ramekins that are appropriate for high temperatures for this recipe. We need the broiling to get the burnt look.

CARAMELIZED BANANA SPLIT

SERVES 4

PREP TIME: 10 minutes

ROASTING TIME:
8–10 minutes

ROASTED BANANAS

2 bananas, not too ripe and unpeeled,
cut in half lengthwise

4 tbsp (60 g) packed light brown sugar,
divided

CARAMEL SAUCE

½ cup (120 ml) sweetened condensed
milk

½ cup (120 ml) heavy cream

¼ cup (60 ml) maple syrup or golden
syrup

2 tbsp (30 g) packed light brown sugar

FOR SERVING

8 scoops best-quality vanilla ice cream

1 cup (100 g) fresh raspberries

4 tbsp (40 g) crushed roasted hazelnuts

Banana splits were our all-time favorite summer dessert growing up. I mean, what is not to love? Sweet, fruity bananas; ice cream; creamy, golden-brown caramel; whipped cream on top; and fresh raspberries or cherries. Basically, it's every child's dream come true. But why would we roast anything for a banana split? Well, baking the bananas with brown sugar takes this dessert to another level. The result is a beautiful caramelization that brings even more flavor to the dish. Serve on a hot summer afternoon, for kids' parties, or for birthday celebrations.

Arrange a rack in the middle of the oven, then preheat it to 430°F (220°C). Line a baking sheet with parchment paper.

For the bananas, sprinkle each cut side of the bananas with 1 tablespoon (15 g) of the brown sugar. Spread the sugar with your hand so that it sticks to the bananas. Place the bananas, sugar side down, on the prepared baking sheet.

Roast the bananas on the middle rack of the oven for 8 to 10 minutes, or until the bananas are caramelized.

While the bananas are roasting, make the caramel sauce. In a saucepan, bring the sweetened condensed milk, cream, maple syrup, and brown sugar to a boil over medium-high heat. Lower the temperature, and, while continually stirring, cook the sauce for 5 to 8 minutes, or until it is brown and slightly thickened. Remove the sauce from the heat, and set it aside to cool.

To serve, remove the bananas from the oven, let them cool for about 5 minutes, then peel them. Carefully lift the bananas from the parchment. Put a banana on each of four plates. Top each banana with two scoops of the ice cream. Drizzle the ice cream with caramel sauce, and top the banana split with the raspberries and hazelnuts.

NOTE: Roasted bananas are very hot, so be careful when taking them out of the oven.

GLAZED PINEAPPLE
with Coconut Cream

The tropical aroma of roasted pineapple is divine. It feels like the pineapple only really comes to life with the process of roasting. It becomes incredibly sweet and juicy, especially when glazed with a citrusy mixture of lime, rum, and vanilla. This beautiful combination should definitely be served with the whipped coconut cream, which gives it an extra exotic flavor and a much-needed lightness and slightly nutty, fresh flavor. Glazed pineapple can be served for breakfast, brunch, a luxurious snack, or a healthy dessert.

ROASTED PINEAPPLE

1 tbsp (15 g) packed light brown sugar

⅛ tsp freshly ground black pepper

1 tsp canola oil

1 large pineapple, peeled, a thin slice cut from the side to flatten it

GLAZE

4 tbsp (60 g) packed light brown sugar

Freshly grated zest and juice of 1 lime

1 tsp vanilla bean paste

2 tbsp (30 ml) white rum

1 pinch of crushed red pepper

½ tsp ground cloves

WHIPPED COCONUT CREAM

½ cup (120 ml) coconut whipping cream

½ cup (120 ml) whipping cream

1 tbsp (15 g) sugar

½ tsp vanilla bean paste

FOR SERVING

Coconut chips, optional

Chopped fresh mint, optional

Arrange a rack in the middle of the oven, then preheat it to 430°F (220°C).

For the pineapple, in a large bowl, rub the brown sugar, pepper, and oil all over the pineapple.

Place the pineapple, cut side down, on a baking sheet. Roast the pineapple on the middle rack of the oven for 10 minutes.

While the pineapple is roasting, make the glaze. In a bowl, stir to combine the brown sugar, lime zest and juice, vanilla bean paste, rum, crushed red pepper, and cloves. When the pineapple has roasted for 10 minutes, remove it from the oven. Brush the pineapple generously with the glaze, and roast for 5 minutes. Repeat the glazing and roasting process two more times, for a total of 15 minutes of additional roasting.

Make the whipped cream while the pineapple is roasting. Using an electric mixer, beat together the coconut whipping cream, whipping cream, sugar, and vanilla bean paste until stiff peaks form.

To serve, remove the pineapple from the oven, and cut it into ½-inch (1-cm)-thick rings. Arrange the pineapple rings on a serving platter. Pour the roasting juices over the pineapple. Top the pineapple with a generous dollop of the whipped cream, and sprinkle it with the coconut chips and mint, if using.

ROASTED BERRIES SUNDAE

SERVES 4

PREP TIME: 5 minutes

ROASTING TIME:
15–20 minutes

1 lb (450 g) frozen mixed berries

3 tbsp (45 g) light brown sugar

Freshly grated zest of 1 lemon

1 tbsp (15 ml) freshly squeezed lemon juice

1 tsp vanilla extract or vanilla seeds

12 scoops vanilla bean ice cream

My (Maja's) big brother and I used to regularly visit a nearby restaurant on Sunday afternoons to order the simplest dessert on the menu: hot, roasted berries with cold vanilla ice cream. We took that hour to bond, laugh, and enjoy a tasty dessert. Little did we know that making it at home is so easy and so quick. It's one of the easiest desserts you can make. You choose the best-possible vanilla bean (or other) ice cream and top it with hot, roasted mixed berries. The ice cream will melt, so you need to dig in quickly and enjoy the magical combination of both worlds.

Arrange a rack in the middle of the oven, then preheat it to 450°F (230°C).

In a large bowl, combine the berries, brown sugar, lemon zest, lemon juice, and vanilla. Spread the mixture over a baking sheet. Roast the berries on the middle rack of the oven for 15 to 20 minutes, or until the berries are tender and their juices are released.

Put three scoops of the ice cream in each of four bowls. Spoon the roasted berries over the ice cream, and serve as quickly as possible.

NOTE: If you use fresh berries for this recipe, reduce the roasting time by 5 minutes.

ROASTED ORANGES
with Whipped Mascarpone

SERVES 4

PREP TIME: 10 minutes

ROASTING TIME:
18–20 minutes

ROASTED ORANGES

6 oranges, peeled
4 tbsp (60 g) packed light brown sugar
2 tbsp (30 ml) white rum
½ tsp vanilla extract

WHIPPED MASCARPONE

2½ cups (350 g) mascarpone
4 tbsp (60 g) sugar
Freshly grated zest of 1 orange
1 tsp vanilla extract
½ cup (120 ml) whipping cream

FOR SERVING

Crushed sfogliatine cookies (see Note)

This simple way to use oranges is probably one of our favorite winter desserts. Roasted oranges release so much juice and flavor that it's truly magical. This dessert has all the delicious components a showstopping dessert should have. It is juicy, sweet, and incredibly rich. The vanilla-scented roasted oranges are full of citrusy flavors, and the creamy whipped mascarpone with orange essence is a lovely light addition. Crushed cookies on top add some texture and extra crunch. We serve this for celebrations, gatherings, or a simple weeknight dessert.

Arrange racks in the middle and at the top of the oven, then preheat it to 450°F (230°C).

Over a bowl, segment the oranges. Arrange the segments in a single layer in a deep, broiler-proof baking dish. Squeeze the juice from the orange membranes over the segments in the dish, and pour in any juice from the bowl. Add the brown sugar, rum, and vanilla, and toss to combine the ingredients.

Roast the oranges for 15 minutes, then transfer the baking dish with the oranges to the top rack. Change the oven temperature to high broil, and broil the oranges for 3 to 5 minutes, or until they are juicy, caramelized, and glossy. Remove the oranges from the oven, and set them aside to cool for 5 to 8 minutes.

While the oranges are roasting, make the whipped mascarpone. In a bowl, using an electric mixer, beat together the mascarpone, sugar, orange zest, vanilla, and whipping cream until it's well combined, about 1 to 2 minutes.

To serve, divide the mascarpone cream among four bowls. Spoon the roasted oranges and roasting juices over the cream, then sprinkle the oranges with the cookies. Serve immediately.

NOTE: Sfogliatine cookies are Italian cookies made from puff pastry dough. They are crispy and light. If you don't have sfogliatine cookies at home, feel free to use crumbled leftover pound cake, brioche bread, or butter cookies.

ROASTED STRAWBERRIES AND CREAM

SERVES 4

PREP TIME: 5 minutes

ROASTING TIME:
12–15 minutes

ROASTED STRAWBERRIES

1 lb (450 g) strawberries, cut in half

1 tsp freshly grated lemon zest

1 tbsp (15 ml) freshly squeezed lemon juice

4 tbsp (60 g) sugar

1 tsp vanilla extract

CREAM

1½ cups (360 ml) whipping cream

1 tbsp (15 g) sugar

½ tsp vanilla extract

FOR SERVING

Chopped fresh lemon balm or mint, optional

Strawberries are the first fruits that welcome us in the early spring in our garden. The first strawberry picked is always so incredibly juicy and sweet. There are endless dessert possibilities when it comes to strawberries: cake, pavlovas, ice cream, and more. However, there is something special about keeping it simple, especially when we are using the first batch of homegrown fruits. Roasted strawberries release juices that are full of flavor and sweetness. Whipped cream adds some lightness and creaminess to the dish. For some extra freshness, we sprinkle this easy, quick dessert with chopped fresh herbs.

Arrange a rack in the middle of the oven, then preheat it to 410°F (210°C).

Put the strawberries in a large bowl. Add the lemon zest and juice, sugar, and vanilla. Stir to combine, then transfer the mixture to a deep baking dish.

Roast the strawberries on the middle rack of the oven for 12 to 15 minutes, or until the strawberries are tender and the baking juices are slightly thickened.

While the strawberries are roasting, whip the cream. In a bowl, whisk the whipping cream with the sugar and vanilla until stiff peaks form, about 3 to 5 minutes.

Remove the strawberries from the oven, and let them cool for 5 minutes.

To serve, divide the roasted strawberries among four bowls. Add a generous dollop of the whipped cream, then sprinkle on the lemon balm, if using.

CARAMELIZED PEARS
with Blackberries and Almonds

SERVES 4–6

PREP TIME: 5 minutes

ROASTING TIME: 20 minutes

We have two old pear trees in our backyard. They are more than 50 years old, yet every year they greet us with the juiciest, most beautiful pears. To celebrate those sweet fruits, we like to roast them, because it brings out the best of their sweetness and fruitiness. The pears get tender but still hold their shape. The blackberries complement them magnificently. Two things make this dish spectacular: roasted sliced almonds on top for crunchiness and a generous dollop of sour cream for creaminess. Serve them warm, and devour this simple pear dish.

PEARS

4 Abate Fetel or Bartlett pears, seeded and cut in half

4 tbsp (55 g) unsalted butter

⅓ cup (80 g) sugar

⅓ cup (80 ml) Moscato, Vin Santo, or white Port

½ tsp vanilla bean paste

Peels of 2 lemons

2 tbsp (30 ml) freshly squeezed lemon juice

1 cup (125 g) blackberries

⅓ cup (25 g) sliced almonds

FOR SERVING

Sour cream or vanilla ice cream

Arrange a rack in the middle of the oven, then preheat it to 450°F (230°C).

Place the pears, cut side up, on a rimmed baking sheet.

In a saucepan, combine the butter, sugar, wine, and vanilla bean paste. Place the saucepan over medium-low heat, and bring the mixture to a boil. Stir, then reduce the heat to low, and simmer the mixture for 5 minutes, or until it's golden brown and reduced by about half. Add the lemon peels, and remove the pan from the heat.

Pour the butter mixture over the pears on the baking sheet. Sprinkle the pears with the lemon juice. Roast the pears for 15 minutes. Remove the pears from the oven, arrange the blackberries over them, and sprinkle the blackberries with the almonds. Roast for 5 minutes, or until the pears are soft, cooked, and caramelized on the outside and the almonds are slightly toasted.

To serve, remove and discard the lemon peels. Divide the roasted pears and blackberries among four to six plates, then drizzle the fruit with the roasting juices. Spoon a dollop of the sour cream on top, and serve immediately.

SPEEDY SOFT DARK CHOCOLATE CAKES

SERVES 6

PREP TIME: 10 minutes

ROASTING TIME: 18–20 minutes

When you crave a delicious chocolate cake, but you really don't feel like spending hours in the kitchen, it is good to have a quick and straightforward recipe that will satisfy your cravings. This chocolate cake is extra soft, fluffy, and delicious, plus it is made in just under 30 minutes. You will need only seven very simple ingredients that you probably already have in your pantry. Serve this cake with a generous scoop of vanilla bean ice cream. And don't forget, the better the quality of the chocolate, the better the cake.

CAKE

½ cup (115 g) unsalted butter

¾ cup (130 g) dark chocolate chips

4 medium eggs

½ cup (120 g) sugar

Pinch of salt

½ cup (65 g) all-purpose flour

1 tbsp (10 g) Dutch process cocoa powder

FOR SERVING

Vanilla ice cream

1 tbsp (10 g) Dutch process cocoa powder

Arrange a rack at the top of the oven, then preheat it to 430°F (220°C). Using butter, grease six 3-inch (8-cm) ramekins, and place them on a baking sheet.

For the cake, in a microwave-safe bowl, heat the butter and chocolate in 20-second intervals, stirring between each interval, until the mixture is melted. Set it aside to cool.

Crack the eggs into a large bowl. Add the sugar and salt. Mix to combine, using an electric mixer for 2 to 3 minutes at high speed, then add the melted chocolate mixture. Mix on high speed for 1 minute. Add the flour and cocoa, and mix until the batter is just combined and smooth.

Spoon the batter evenly into the ramekins. Roast the cake on the top rack of the oven for 18 to 20 minutes, or until a toothpick inserted into the center of each cake comes out clean.

To serve, top the warm or room-temperature cakes with a scoop of the ice cream and sprinkle with the cocoa powder.

SALTED CARAMEL NUTS

SERVES 4

PREP TIME: 10 minutes

ROASTING TIME:
6–8 minutes

2 cups (240 g) mixed nuts, such as
almonds, pecans, walnuts, hazelnuts,
and peanuts
1 cup (240 g) sugar
⅓ cup (80 ml) water
1 tbsp (15 ml) honey
½ tsp fleur de sel
1 tsp vanilla bean paste
Salt

Oh my, the aroma from homemade caramel spreading through the house is better than any scented candle burning. It is sweet, homey, and hearty. Caramelized nuts remind us of our childhood. They make the perfect homemade snack. I mean, who would complain about crunchy nuts coated in salted caramel and broken into clusters? Enjoy these nuts as a snack, sprinkle them over vanilla ice cream for dessert, or add them to your breakfast granola. You can easily store them, in an airtight container at room temperature, for up to 1 month.

Arrange a rack in the middle of the oven, then preheat it to 390°F (200°C). Line a baking sheet with a silicone mat or parchment paper.

Spread the mixed nuts in a single layer on the prepared baking sheet.

Roast the nuts on the middle rack of the oven for 6 to 8 minutes, or until they are nicely toasted.

While the nuts are roasting, prepare the caramel. Add the sugar, water, and honey to a saucepan, and place it over medium-high heat. Bring the mixture to a boil, and cook it for 5 to 8 minutes, or until it's golden brown, stirring occasionally. Be careful; the caramel is very hot. Remove the caramel from the heat, add the fleur de sel and vanilla bean paste, mix well, and pour the caramel evenly over the nuts. Make sure all of the nuts are covered. Sprinkle them with salt.

When the salted caramel nuts are cooled, break them into clusters with your hands. Breaking them in larger clusters enhances the crispiness.

NOTE: For easier cleaning, fill the saucepan from cooking the caramel with water. Place all of the metal utensils in the saucepan, and bring the water to a boil over medium-low heat. Simmer the water for a few minutes, then pour out the hot water from the saucepan, and clean the metal utensils and the pan.

ESSENTIAL SAUCES

In this chapter, you will find the quickest recipes, most needing only five minutes to make. But don't think that just because these recipes are quick to make they aren't important. A good sauce can transform a dish from OK to pure perfection. So take that extra 5 minutes and make the most delicious sauce for your roast.

For all the spicy food lovers, try the Salsa Roja (page 229) or Roasted Garlic and Lemon Mayonnaise (page 231). Hollandaise sauce lovers will adore the simple Béarnaise Sauce (page 230). You can take vegetables, kebabs, chicken, and fish to the next level with the smoky, rich Turkish Roasted Red Pepper Dip (page 235). Last, but not least, don't forget to make the classic Gravy (page 226) every time you make steak or delicious meat roasts.

GRAVY

A simple gravy recipe is one of the most important ones to have, if you ask me. It can elevate a steak from good to extremely delicious. Making gravy is easy, but make sure to choose the right semisweet wine, or the gravy may taste sour instead of perfectly balanced. Serve this gravy with pork, chicken, or beef.

GRAVY

2 tbsp (28 g) unsalted butter

1½ tbsp (15 g) all-purpose flour

1 shallot, diced

½ tsp tomato paste

1½ cups (360 ml) chicken or beef stock

1 bay leaf or sprig of fresh thyme

2 tbsp (30 ml) white Port, Sherry, or Riesling, optional

1 tsp Worcestershire sauce or Maggi sauce

2 tbsp (30 ml) heavy cream

FOR SERVING

Chopped fresh herbs, optional

1 tbsp (15 g) cranberry or lingonberry jam, optional

Place a saucepan with the butter, flour, shallot, and tomato paste over medium-low heat. Stir, and cook for 5 minutes, or until the mixture is lightly browned. Stir in the chicken stock, bay leaf, wine, if using, and Worcestershire. Bring the mixture to a boil, while constantly stirring. Reduce the heat and simmer for 5 to 10 minutes, stirring occasionally, until the gravy is smooth and thick.

Add the heavy cream, and stir to combine it with the gravy. Bring the gravy to a boil, then remove it from the heat. Stir in the herbs and cranberry jam, if using.

HONEY MUSTARD SAUCE

SERVES 4

PREP TIME: 5 minutes

⅓ cup (80 ml) mayonnaise
¼ cup (60 ml) yellow American mustard
1 tbsp (15 ml) apple cider vinegar
¼ cup (60 ml) honey
Salt and freshly ground black pepper

This sauce is not only the easiest, but it's also the perfect addition to roasted chicken or pork. There are only four ingredients in this recipe, not counting salt and pepper, and you simply stir to combine everything in a bowl. That's it; it doesn't get any easier.

In a bowl, stir to combine the mayonnaise, mustard, vinegar, and honey. Season to taste with salt and pepper.

BREAD AND HORSERADISH SAUCE

SERVES 4

PREP TIME: 6 minutes

1 slice sourdough bread, crusts removed and bread cut into cubes
½ cup (40 g) grated horseradish
½ cup (120 ml) sour cream
1 tbsp (15 ml) apple cider vinegar
Salt and freshly ground black pepper

In Slovenia, we eat horseradish for Easter, so this is a wonderful sauce to enjoy in the spring. The sauce goes tremendously well with roasted beef, game, and chicken. It's slightly spicy and full of flavor, yet fresh, creamy, and easy to make.

In a small bowl, cover the bread with lukewarm water, and soak it for 5 minutes. Drain the water from the bread.

In a bowl, stir to combine the bread, horseradish, and sour cream. Stir in the vinegar, and season the sauce with salt and pepper.

SALSA ROJA

3 ripe tomatoes

¼ medium-sized onion

2 cloves garlic

1 tbsp (15 ml) apple cider vinegar

½ fresh chile, such as serrano or jalapeño

3 sprigs cilantro

1 tbsp (15 ml) olive oil

Salt and freshly ground black pepper

Thanks to the serrano pepper or jalapeño, this is the spiciest sauce in this book. Serving this salsa as a side for roasted steak, fish, chicken, or vegetables will make spicy food lovers happy.

In a blender, combine the tomatoes, onion, garlic, vinegar, chile, cilantro, and oil. Blend for 2 minutes, until you get a smooth sauce.

Transfer the sauce to a saucepan. Place the pan over medium-low heat, then bring the mixture to a boil, and boil it for 10 minutes. Remove the salsa from the heat, and season it with salt and pepper to taste. The salsa can be served warm or at room temperature.

BÉARNAISE SAUCE

SERVES 4

PREP TIME: 5 minutes

¾ cup (170 g) unsalted butter

2 eggs

2 tbsp (30 ml) freshly squeezed lemon juice

Salt and freshly ground black pepper

Pinch of cayenne pepper

2 tbsp (10 g) chopped fresh chives or tarragon

A classic French sauce, béarnaise is very similar to hollandaise sauce, but with the addition of fresh herbs. It's easy to make and perfect to serve with fish, chicken, vegetables, or eggs. Make sure to prepare enough, because it's impossible to resist.

Bring the butter to a boil in a saucepan set over medium-high heat. In a blender, combine the eggs and lemon juice. Season with salt, pepper, and the cayenne. With the blender running, gradually pour in the boiling-hot melted butter in a thin stream, until it's combined and the sauce is smooth. Transfer the sauce to a bowl, then stir in the chives, and season to taste with additional salt and pepper.

ROASTED GARLIC AND LEMON MAYONNAISE

SERVES 6

PREP TIME: 5 minutes

ROASTING TIME:
20–25 minutes

ROASTED GARLIC AND LEMON

½ garlic bulb, cut in half

½ lemon

1 tsp olive oil

Salt and freshly ground black pepper

MAYONNAISE

1 large egg yolk

1 tsp Dijon mustard

½ tsp apple cider vinegar

¼ cup (60 ml) olive oil

¾ cup (180 ml) sunflower or vegetable oil

Pinch of cayenne pepper

Salt and freshly ground black pepper

Making mayonnaise at home is just the easiest thing ever, and it will only take about a minute to put it together. It is the queen of all condiments. It is incredibly delicious, creamy, full of flavor, and a must on burgers, sandwiches, and as a side with Sweet Potato Fries (page 167). Adding roasted garlic and roasted lemon juice to the mayonnaise gives it character and a deep Mediterranean flavor.

Arrange a rack in the middle of the oven, then preheat it to 430°F (220°C).

For the garlic and lemon, scrunch up some parchment paper and run it under water to soak it. Drizzle the garlic and lemon with the olive oil, and season them with salt and pepper. Wrap the garlic and lemon in the wet parchment paper, and then in aluminum foil.

Place the foil packet on a baking sheet and place on the middle rack of the oven for 20 to 25 minutes, or until the garlic is soft and easily removed from the skin. Unwrap the garlic and lemon, and set them aside.

While the garlic is roasting, make the mayonnaise. In a glass jar, use an immersion blender to combine the egg yolk, mustard, and vinegar. (The mayonnaise can also be made in a food processor.)

In a measuring cup or pitcher, combine the olive and sunflower oils. In a thin stream gradually add the oil to the mayonnaise mixture, while continually blending or running the food processor motor. You will see the mayonnaise start to thicken after about a quarter of the oil has been incorporated. Continue adding the oil, while continually blending, until you get a nice, creamy, thick mayonnaise.

Squeeze the garlic flesh from the skin, and stir it into the mayonnaise. Squeeze the juice from the roasted lemon and stir it in. Add the cayenne, salt, and pepper, and stir. The mayonnaise may be kept, refrigerated, for up to 1 week.

*See photo on page 224.

NOTE: If using store-bought mayonnaise, combine the mayonnaise, a pinch of cayenne, and 2 tablespoons (30 ml) of olive oil. Then, squeeze in the garlic and lemon juice, as above.

ROMESCO SAUCE

2 roasted red bell peppers from a jar

1 clove garlic

2 tbsp (10 g) parsley leaves

¾ cup (80 g) slivered almonds, toasted

2 tbsp (30 g) tomato passata or tomato puree

1 tbsp (15 ml) sherry vinegar

½ tsp paprika

½ tsp cayenne pepper

⅓ cup (80 ml) olive oil

Salt and freshly ground black pepper

This Spanish sauce celebrates ripe tomatoes and peppers. It's a fresh, light, and slightly spicy sauce, perfect for roasted cauliflower, chicken, and pork. Store in an airtight container, in the fridge, for up to 14 days.

In a blender or food processor, mix the roasted red peppers, garlic, parsley, almonds, passata, vinegar, paprika, and cayenne. Pulse a couple of times to get a creamy, smooth sauce. Add the olive oil, pulse to combine it, then season to taste with salt and pepper.

PEANUT BUTTER SAUCE

SERVES 4

PREP TIME: 5 minutes

ROASTING TIME:
8–10 minutes

1 cup (150 g) peanuts

2 tbsp (30 ml) light soy sauce

¼ cup (60 ml) canola oil

2 tbsp (30 ml) rice vinegar

1 tbsp (15 g) chili paste, such as
sambal oelek

1 tbsp (15 ml) honey

½ cup (120 ml) water

¼ tsp salt

1 clove garlic

1-inch (2-cm) piece ginger, sliced

Peanut butter lovers will adore this sauce. Roasted peanuts are aromatic, and they release a lot of flavorful oils that enrich this simple sauce. Serve this sauce with chicken or pork, or use it as a dip for roasted vegetables.

Arrange a rack in the middle of the oven, then preheat it to 410°F (210°C).

Spread the peanuts in a single layer on a baking sheet. Roast the peanuts on the middle rack of the oven for 8 to 10 minutes, or until they are lightly toasted. Let the peanuts cool for a few minutes.

In a blender, combine the roasted peanuts, soy sauce, oil, vinegar, chili paste, honey, water, salt, garlic, and ginger. Mix for 3 to 5 minutes, until you get a smooth, creamy sauce.

GREMOLATA SAUCE

SERVES 4

PREP TIME: 5 minutes

2 cloves garlic, diced

2 tbsp (30 ml) freshly squeezed lemon juice

3 tbsp (45 ml) olive oil

1 tbsp (15 ml) canola oil

Salt and freshly ground black pepper

¼ tsp crushed red pepper

3 tbsp (15 g) chopped fresh parsley or cilantro

We always make gremolata from scratch when we eat fish at home. Originating from Italy, this simple sauce is made from garlic, lemon juice, high-quality olive oil, and herbs. Serve it with fish, steak, or chicken or spooned over vegetables.

In a bowl, stir to combine the garlic, lemon juice, olive oil, and canola oil. Season with salt and pepper, then stir in the crushed red pepper and parsley.

TURKISH ROASTED RED PEPPER DIP

⅓ cup (40 g) walnuts

Roasted peppers (page 182)

1 clove garlic

¼ tsp ground cumin

½ tsp dried oregano

½ tsp ground coriander

¼ tsp dried mint

¼ tsp crushed red pepper

Salt and freshly ground black pepper

2 tbsp (30 ml) olive oil

1 tsp pomegranate molasses

1 tbsp (6 g) breadcrumbs

If you love roasted peppers, then you will love this incredibly rich, slightly smoky and aromatic Turkish dip. Serve it with vegetables, kebabs, chicken, and fish, as a dip or a sauce. Store in an airtight container, in the fridge, for up to 14 days.

In a food processor or a blender, mix the walnuts, roasted red peppers, garlic, cumin, oregano, coriander, mint, crushed red pepper, salt and pepper, oil, molasses, and breadcrumbs. Pulse for a few times to get a creamy red bell pepper dip.

ROASTED SESAME SEED PASTE

SERVES 6

PREP TIME: 10 minutes

ROASTING TIME: 5–8 minutes

1 cup (144 g) sesame seeds
⅓ cup (80 ml) canola oil

Making tahini at home is super easy, and you will need only two simple ingredients. Make it creamy and use it in spreads, salad dressings, and marinades. Store in an airtight container, in the fridge, for up to 3 months.

Arrange a rack in the middle of the oven, then preheat it to 390°F (200°C).

Spread the sesame seeds in a single layer over a baking sheet. Roast the seeds for 5 minutes, or until they are lightly toasted but not brown. Roast the seeds for 2 to 3 minutes longer if you prefer a darker color and more tart tahini.

Remove the seeds from the oven, and transfer them to a food processor or blender while they are still hot. Pulse on high speed until a smooth paste forms, about 5 minutes.

Transfer the sesame seed paste to a bowl. Add the canola oil and mix until combined.

Acknowledgments

There is a huge leap from having an idea for a book to having it published. There are so many people involved in the process, and we are forever grateful to all of you for your encouragement and support.

First of all, we would like to thank our editor, Lauren, for giving us the opportunity to write our very first book. Thank you for all of your assistance, support, feedback, and compromise. A big thank-you to everyone on the Page Street Publishing team for all of your hard work and excellent communication.

Thanks to Adam, for being our ray of sunshine and keeping us motivated during the process of making our first book.

To our parents, Zalika, Darinka, Srecko, and Milan: Thank you for your patience, grocery shopping, everyday recipe testing, and tasting. Thank you for always being our biggest cheerleaders, and, lastly, thank you for your moral support. Thank you, Anja (and your family), for always being such a positive soul and for your willingness to help with recipe testing.

Special thanks to our best friends for your support, interest, and cheerleading.

This book wouldn't be possible without our readers and food community. You guys are the kindest people, and your comments and recreations of our recipes always encourage us to be better for you.

Thanks to our neighbors and family members for always willingly testing recipes and for all of your honest feedback. It helped us so much with recipe development and making these recipes foolproof.

Last but not least, thanks to our local butcher for going the extra mile and providing us with the best cuts of meat for this book. We truly appreciate it.

About the Authors

Maja and Jernej Zver are founders of a popular Slovenian food blog, Jernej Kitchen, which won The Best Slovenian Food Blog award in 2016, as well as the Foodie Influencer award in 2019.

Jernej attended culinary school, and he was able to work with numerous renowned chefs in restaurants. He now works as a recipe developer and food stylist. Maja is a designer who specializes in food photography. Together, Maja and Jernej run their food blog.

Their work has been featured in countless web and print publications, including My Domaine, PureWow, The Everygirl, Martha Stewart, *Shape*, Bake from Scratch, *Elle*, *Cosmopolitan*, and many others. They work and live in Slovenia.

Visit them at jernejkitchen.com, or follow along on Instagram, @jernejkitchen.

Index